P9-DHI-173

AMERICAN DATING ASSOCIATION

"The Official Governing Body of Courtship

in the United States"

Universal Dating
Regulations & Bylaws

A Fireside Book
Published by Simon & Schuster

New York   London   Toronto   Sydney   Singapore

FIRESIDE
Rockefeller Center
1230 Avenue of the Americas
New York, NY 10020

Copyright © 2001 by Jeff Wise
All rights reserved,
including the right of reproduction
in whole or in part in any form.

FIRESIDE and colophon are registered trademarks
of Simon & Schuster Inc.

Designed by Ruth Lee

Manufactured in the United States of America

10   9   8   7   6   5   4   3   2   1

Library of Congress Cataloging-in-Publication Data

   Universal dating regulations & bylaws : the official governing body of
courtship in the United States / American Dating Association.
        p. cm.
     "A Fireside book."
     1. Dating—Humor   I. Title: Universal dating regulations and bylaws.
   PN6231.D3 U55   2001
   306.73'02'07—dc21

                                                    00-046270

ISBN 0-7432-0056-X

The American Dating Association is intended as a support mechanism for trau-
matized unwed heterosexuals and is not a licensed medical or psychological
counseling institution. Any advice given should be acted upon at the discretion
of each individual in an adult, responsible manner. The American Dating Association, the ADA Web site, and the *Universal Dating Regulations & Bylaws* are for
entertainment purposes only and not to be used as a navigational device.

To the countless American single people, past and present, who, by dint of their steadfast dedication to the principles of dating compliance, have helped make courtship a safer, saner, and more life-affirming activity.

Contents

Welcome

Hello, and welcome to the twenty-fifth edition of the American Dating Association's *Universal Dating Regulations & Bylaws*. As we at the ADA celebrate our first quarter century—and the official beginning of the third millennium—we also lift our champagne flutes to acknowledge the dawning of a new era of responsible dating practices.

It seems like only yesterday that dating in the United States was a wholly unregulated, unsupervised activity. Thanks to the pioneering efforts of our founder, Dr. Rutger Fury, and to a dedicated team of relationship professionals across the country, that picture has changed dramatically.

Now boasting a membership of 2.5 million in the United States and abroad, the American Dating Assocation continues to grow year to year. Its advisory boards include more than five hundred of the nation's foremost experts in the fields of psychology, sociology, psychiatry, law, sexology, and medicine. Behind all of our efforts is a single, simple goal: promoting sensible, safe, and sane dating behavior.

Enormous challenges remain ahead. For far too long, dating has been viewed as a minor, benighted, halfway stage between the asexuality of childhood and the monumental commitment of marriage. In the last twenty-five years, however, single Americans from every walk of life have begun standing together to claim their rights as full human beings, worthy of respect and needful of recognition. We at the ADA stand with them to declare that dating is a noble and worthwhile pursuit in its own right, regardless of any particular relationship's outcome.

As president of the ADA, I have had many occasions to witness the damage that poor dating practices can wreak. For far too many people in our country, dating can be an exercise in denial: getting into relationships even though you know they're wrong, or enduring bad behavior and telling yourself that it really doesn't matter. But unacceptable behavior does matter, and its ultimate effect is a trail of hurt and woe.

At the end of the day, no one can stand up for your rights but you. But the ADA is here to help you identify your rights and to clarify your range of options. Our services are manyfold. Perhaps best known is the Green Book, which you hold in your hand. Published for a quarter century, it is a rigorous compilation of what daters may or may not do in the course of a premarital relationship. With the Green Book, each and every dater can have a portable, instantly accessible database that allows him or her to self-arbitrate any dating-related dispute.

Since 1998, the "new" ADA has strived mightily to remake itself into a more accessible, more proactive organization so that it might better keep in touch with the needs of its membership. One of its major initiatives has been to expand and modernize the Rogue Dater Advisory Service, which is now available online at our recently expanded Web site, www.americandating.org. Via this service, members across the country can identify and avoid the worst of the nation's serial dating offenders. In addition, any member who believes that he or she has been the victim of a callous and cruel dater can nominate this erstwhile partner as a Rogue Dater. If the nomination is accepted, the dater in question will be fed into the alert system.

Another service now offered via our website is ADA Dating Arbitration, which helps members identify and resolve dating-related crises. This ever-popular service has recently been modified and streamlined, so that daters in trouble-stricken relationships can get the help they need more quickly and effectively than ever.

This year, we are continuing our highly successful National Outreach program, which has boosted individual memberships by 30 percent over the last three years. As part of this program, for the first time ever we will be distributing the Green Book through standard retail channels, including bookstores. We would like to thank Fireside, a division of Simon & Schuster, for their partnership in this initiative.

In closing, I would like to thank you for your interest in the American Dating Association and its services and products. And, if you are not already a member, I would like to invite you to come stand together with us as part of our "team." Our philosophy is simple. The more people understand the rules of courtship, the fewer people will be needlessly hurt.

That's a mission we're proud of, a mission we stand behind every day.

Sincerely,

Jerome Smiley
President, American Dating
    Association

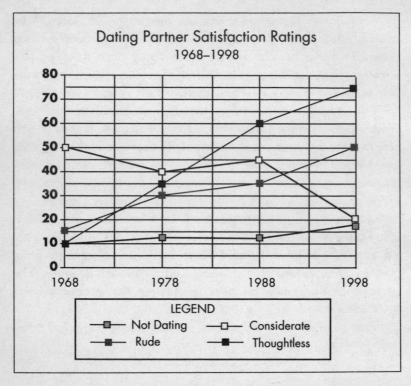

Fig. 1. Dating Partner Satisfaction Ratings. Groups of 1,000 single American women were polled as to whether they were in relationships, and, if so, how they would characterize the behavior of their partners. The data show that, over a thirty-year period, the percentage of boyfriends rated "considerate" has fallen from 60 percent to 28 percent, while the percentage rated "thoughtless" has risen from 8 percent to 58 percent. Such evidence corroborates a general decline in dating behavior. *Data from ADA Cross-Sectional Demographic Survey #876, August 1999.*

A Brief History of the "Green Book"

The year was 1969. Man was walking on the moon; the New York Mets were clinching the World Series title for the first time ever. And all across the country, single Americans were experimenting with unprecedented levels of sexual and emotional freedom. It was a wild time. A crazy time. A historic time.

And for pioneering relationship psychologist Dr. Rutger Fury, a time of both crisis and opportunity. As one of the nation's foremost experts on heterosexual courtship, Dr. Fury witnessed firsthand the extreme stresses that the "sexual revolution" had placed on young men and women.

"When our work began," Dr. Fury later recalled in his best-selling autobiography, *It Takes Two to Tango,* "virtually every subject we talked to seemed to have his or her own opinion as to what constituted acceptable behavior during dating. In a time of great social upheaval, there were many incompatible, even contradictory, notions floating about. It was clear that order had to be established."

Then a researcher at Harvard University, Dr. Fury relinquished his prestigious chair to throw himself headlong into the personal and professional odyssey that would ultimately reshape the face of dating studies. Sensing that the fault lines then shaking the culture could most closely be studied on the West Coast, Dr. Fury moved to Sacramento, California, and founded the Greater Sacramento Human Relationship Initiative. Bringing together resources from government, academia, and private benefactors, the GSHRI became a test bed of private/public sector cooperation. In 1973 it received a charter from the California State Senate at a ceremony in which Secretary of State Jerry Brown praised "the bold innovation which lies at the heart of this unique endeavor."

This official recognition gave the GSHRI's work an important boost at a critical juncture. Thanks to the social upheavals and "sexual

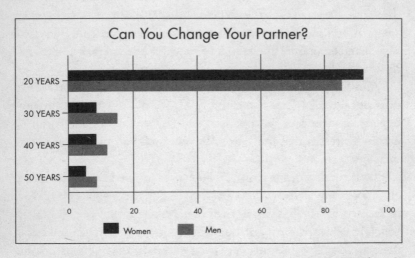

Fig. 2. Perceived Malleability of Mate Psychoschematics. Four cadres of single and married couples were identified, in the age ranges of 19–21, 29–31, 39–41, and 49–51, and asked if they felt they could change undesirable features of their partners' character. Male and female responses correlated closely across all age ranges. The most striking feature of the data is that while few in the older cadres saw any hope for changing their partners, a large majority of young respondents felt it was possible. *Source: American Dating Association Biannual Psychostatistical Gazette, 1999/2000.*

revolution" of the late '60s and early '70s, American society had undergone an unprecedented transformation in the types of dating opportunities available to the average man and woman. Responsibility, however, did not always go hand in hand with freedom. Reported cases of callous, thoughtless, and even intentionally cruel dating behavior had skyrocketed.

Something had to be done—and the GSHRI answered the call, taking the first steps in a massive project that would eventually become the Universal Dating Regulations & Bylaws. The mission: to identify, codify, and publish society's heretofore unwritten rules of acceptable courtship behavior. Researchers fanned out across the country, seeking to establish the acceptable standards of practice for every imaginable dating-related scenario.

By 1975 the GSHRI project had ballooned to embrace more than three hundred professional researchers working in all but two of the fifty states. Recognizing that the true scope of the organization's work lay on a national level, Dr. Fury successfully led a drive to transform the Initiative into a truly continent-wide entity, the American Dating Association. In February 1976, the ADA charter was signed by President Gerald Ford in an Oval Office ceremony attended by fourteen state governors, nine university presidents, and a triumphant Dr. Fury.

That momentous year also saw the publication, after years of intensive effort, of the association's first edition of *Universal Dating Regulations & Bylaws*. A twelve-volume, seven-million-word opus, the 1976 *UDR&B* fulfilled its objective of codifying every conceivable dating-related situation. That first year, more than seven hundred complete volumes were printed and sold, mostly to research institutes, universities, and public libraries.

In subsequent years, sales of the *UDR&B* climbed steadily, topping two thousand copies by 1979. But for the man who had started it all, ADA chairman Dr. Fury, steady growth just wasn't good enough. "What I am seeking," he told the annual meeting of ADA researchers in the fall of 1979, "is a way to put the fruits of our institutional labor into the hands of everyone who desires it."

Thus began a five-year effort to find a way to somehow miniaturize and mass-produce the massive knowledge base that made up the *UDR&B*. The solution eventually arrived at was so simple and elegant that in retrospect it seemed obvious: to edit down the vast tracts of legalese into a single, slim, lightweight, and readable volume small enough to fit into the average back pocket. Voilà: The UDR&B Pocket Edition—better known today as the Green Book, after its distinctive cover—was born.

Upon its first publication in February 1985, the Green Book quickly climbed the best-seller charts, where it remained in the number one spot in the "Advice, How-to, and Miscellaneous" category for forty-seven weeks. Today the Green Book remains the best-selling book of its kind, and the fourth-best-selling book of all time.

In its impact upon dating practices in the United States, the book's effects were no less than revolutionary. Thanks to the Green Book, no longer could the raffish rogue carelessly break a heart and then claim, "Hey, I thought it was okay."

"It was like a drop of rain in a parched desert," recalls retired relationship therapist Jerry Moonly, who witnessed the book's initial impact. "We were all shocked by the huge demand that the Green Book generated."

The work of the ADA is hardly complete, however. On the contrary, its mission is more pressing than ever. In a chaotic and unsupervised dating environment, the feelings of unmarried heterosexuals are being trampled in unprecedented numbers. A recent ADA survey revealed that 89 percent of all single people would rather undergo a wisdom tooth extraction without anesthesia than repeat their most painful dating experience. The ADA believes that it can help ease their suffering, and, as ever, it stands ready to meet their needs.

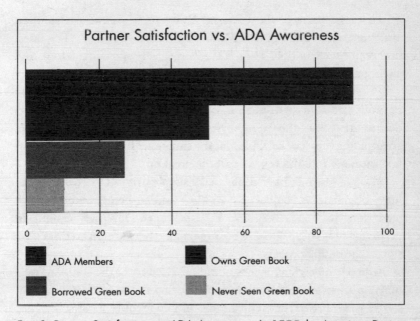

Fig. 3. Partner Satisfaction vs. ADA Awareness. In 1995 the American Dating Assocation Research Division conducted a random phone survey of 1,200 single Americans. A respondent's level of satisfaction with his or her dating companion was found to correlate highly with the degree of familiarity with the American Dating Association and its products. This can be interpreted as indicating that the ADA helps improve relationships and/or perception of said relationships. Alternatively, people who are predisposed to harmonious relationships may also be predisposed to joining organizations like the ADA. *Data from ADA Institutional Normative Database Survey #343, June 2000.*

"As long as there are single people," says Association President Jerome Smiley, "there will be the ADA."

How to Use This Book

First-time users of the *Universal Dating Regulations & Bylaws* often ask, "Just what kind of book is this, and how do I use it?" The question is an excellent one. The *UDR&B* is, strictly speaking, a tool, and its proper use requires handling as such.

Part field manual, part legal codification, the *UDR&B* is a highly rigorous and concise distillation of acceptable American dating practices at the turn of the twenty-first century. Within its pages are rules governing every conceivable dating situation, from the moment of first meeting until the very end of the breakup.

Years of research have confirmed a simple truth: If there is a way to hurt, humiliate, or embarrass another human being, someone will have done it. That's why the ADA has been extremely careful, in preparing the Green Book, to ensure that its users are covered at every step of the dating process.

The central eight chapters of the *UDR&B* cover the standard relationship arc in chronological fashion. To find the ADA regulation that relates to your current predicament, simply identify what stage your relationship is in and then turn to the corresponding chapter. Are you confused as to whether you and your companion are spending time together as platonic buddies or as potential life-mates? You're in the initial noncommittal stage of the relationship; turn to Section IV, "Early Courtship." Bothered because he's moved into your apartment, but still hasn't introduced you to his parents? You're suffering a confusion about commitment often experienced by cohabiters; turn to Section VIII, "Living Together."

The size, shape, and materials of the Green Book have all been carefully chosen to maximize portability and ease of use. In fact, tests show that the current edition is capable of being carried in the back pocket of 93 percent of all trousers sold in the United States. We here at the American Dating Association encourage all *UDR&B* users to carry the book with them at all times, even when they don't expect a traditional "dating" situation to spring up in the near future. Remember: You can't use this book if you don't have it with you.

Important Changes Since Our Last Edition

As society continues to evolve and change, so do its unspoken laws about what is acceptable while dating. Each year, then, the new edition of the Green Book is updated to add newly relevant material and eliminate sections that are no longer in keeping with the spirit of the times.

Among the more significant changes incorporated into the *2000 Universal Dating Regulations & Bylaws:*

- It is no longer considered unacceptable to make or receive a cell phone call during a dinner date. One still may not make or receive cell phone calls, or indeed any type of phone call, during foreplay or sex.
- Email, pagers, and instant messaging have been added to the list of media which are not acceptable for the purposes of informing your partner that you are breaking up with him or her.

**Dating Haiku
"Pulse and Plenitude"**

Passing on the street
I nod, wondering if it's you
Or a lookalike

—G. Laurencia Bigelow,
A Dream of New Beginnings,
Firelight Publishing,
Seattle, 1997

- It is no longer necessary for couples to discuss recent AIDS tests before going to bed together for the first time.

Corrections

Due to editing errors, several mistakes were inadvertently incorporated into the *2000 Universal Dating Regulations & Bylaws*. The American Dating Association apologizes for any inconvenience or misunderstanding that may have been caused.

- Page 15: the phrase "shall be tested by the insertion of a hot fork" should have read "shall not be tested by the insertion of any sharp object, including a hot fork, under any circumstances."
- Page 123: the phrase "clitoris, labia minora, and labia majora" should have read "Thursdays, Tuesdays, and Wednesdays."
- Page 258: the ADA wishes to stress that, except when specific precedent-setting cases are being cited, all names used in examples are fictitious. In particular, the example involving a woman who comes home to find her boyfriend applying hot-oil treatment to her cat was in no way meant to refer to any real-life couple who happened to be named Mark and Diane.

Universal Dating
Regulations & Bylaws

Section I:
Definitions

OVERVIEW: As Alice said in Through the Looking-Glass, "I mean what I say, and I say what I mean." But what do words mean? Commonly, daters in the United States can have very different ideas of what terms mean. In order to minimize misunderstandings and hurt feelings, it's essential that everyone be on the same page about words and their meanings.

act of God, *n.* Any circumstance so wildly beyond the bounds of normative human experience that one cannot be held accountable for one's resultant behavior. *Example 1: Cannibalism, though regarded as one of the least negotiable of all taboos, might be forgiven if one is starving to death amid the plane wreckage atop an Andean mountaintop and half the soccer team is dead, anyway. Example 2: It is wildly improbable that one might become stuck in an elevator with Rebecca Romijn. It is doubly improbable that she would, under such circumstances, be romantically inclined. Therefore, if the two improbabilities were to coincide, it is expecting too much of a man to maintain preexisting promises of fidelity.*

ambiguity, *n.* A state of vagueness or uncertainty regarding one's intentions, generally maintained for the purpose of maximizing one's future options and minimizing one's exposure to embarrassment. *(Note: While ambiguity is an unavoidable feature of an early dating relationship, it is noncompliant to deliberately maximize it.) Usage: "Half the time Amelia is calling me her best buddy, and the other half she's shooting me smoldering looks. The ambiguity is killing me."*

bitch, *v.* To complain in an unwarranted manner, especially when said complaint is produced as a smoke screen to conceal that one is actually angry about something else, but one is hoping the other party will realize of his own accord what the true source of irritation is and take steps to correct it. Cf. "moan," "rag."

bitch, *n.* 1. An unpleasant woman. 2. [hip-hop] A fellow held in low esteem. 3. [hip-hop] Girlfriend. *NB: Generally, language stylists feel that white men should avoid using this word in sense 2 or 3 unless they either have actual African-American lineage or have secured a major-label record contract.*

break up, *v.* To end a dating relationship. *Usage note: The term "break up" is only applied in situations involving people who have explicitly agreed that they are "dating." People who are only "seeing" each other are not technically dating, so they cannot break up.* See also "terminate."

climax, *n.* [poetic] Orgasm.

close, *adj.* Near, a short distance away from. In relationships, sympathetically attached and on a mutual wavelength.

close, *v.* 1. In general terms, to take a potential deal all the way through to its logical conclusion, as when a salesman convinces a prospect to buy his product. 2. On a date, to have sex with one's partner, especially for the first time. *Usage: "He's a bulldog, unstoppable, never quits until he gets what he wants. Yes, that Chuck is a real closer."*

**Dating Haiku
"Memories of You"**

Under the sofa
Two pennies, a big lint ball
And your old lighter

—G. Laurencia Bigelow,
A View from Twilight, Firelight
Publishing, Seattle, 2000

---

compliant, *adj.* Fulfilling the obligations imposed by society on all its members, specifically as enumerated in the American Dating Association's *Universal Dating Regulations & Bylaws.* Ant.: Noncompliant. Cf. "obligation." *Usage: "Hillary was a sweet girl, and totally compliant—until she got drunk one night and violated half the* UDR&B."

compliment, *n.* 1. A heartfelt expression of appreciation for another person's phys-

Stat Attack

America's most popular compliments:

By men:
1. Babe, you look so hot!
2. Ouch!
3. You are smoking!
4. I wanna get a piece of you!
5. No, of course I think you're smart. Yes, I do. All the time. What are you talking about? I tell you that all the time.

By women:
1. That shirt looks good on you.
2. Your haircut looks good.
3. I like those pants better.
4. You look so nice in a sweater.
5. You look handsome in that belt.

Source: "He Says, She Says: A Statistical Synthesis of Psychosexual Belief Modalities," American Dating Association Press, 1999.

ical or mental qualities, appearance, or possessions. 2. A statement made in an attempt to ingratiate oneself into another's favor, especially in pursuit of romantic involvement. 3. A ritualistic form of verbal submission made on a daily basis by men to their female partners.

date, *n.* A period of time spent by one man and one woman in one another's exclusive company, with the implied or explicit intention of investigating future sexual compatibility.

date, *v.* 1. To have sexual intercourse with. 2. To frequently spend time with another person with whom one shares a mutual romantic interest. 3. To share with another person a relationship which both parties have agreed to identify as "dating." *(Note: See* UDR&B *Sec. V.A.)*

double sigma, *n.* 1. In statistics, the cumulative mass of data lying within two standard deviations of the median in a bell-curve distribution, including approximately 95 percent of a randomized data field. 2. In relationship science, an event, fact, or circumstance which can be shown to have occurred, yet which falls so far beyond the statistical norm as to be irrelevant for the formulation of general principles. *Example: Bob has a blind dinner date with Mary, then asks that she split the bill. Regardless, she agrees to have sex with him later that evening (see "Dutch treat," below). This occurrence is deemed a double sigma because it is so wildly improbable.*

Dutch treat, *n.* An informal method among two people of settling a bill, especially one pertaining to a meal, snack, or beverage, in which man and woman pay an equal share. *NB: When deployed on a first date, this system signals to both parties that all future relations shall remain on a strictly platonic basis, and that sexual relations shall never occur. (Note: See* UDR&B *Sec. III.A.vi.e.3.)*

ex, *n.* Gender-neutral abbreviation for "ex-girlfriend" or "ex-boyfriend," i.e., a person with whom one once enjoyed a dating relationship, but no longer does. *NB: A person is not considered an ex unless both parties are currently aware that the dating relationship has been terminated. (Note: See* UDR&B *Sec. IX, "Termination.")*

exclusive, *adj.* Describing a right extended only to one's relationship partner and not to anyone else, ever, not even for a short time or because it "just happened."

frequently, *adv.* 1. At every conceivable opportunity. 2. Every day. 3. Several times a week. 4. More than once a year. 5. Ever.

friend, *n.* 1. A person with whom one is on warm and familiar terms, but with whom one has not had sex. 2. A person with whom one is currently having sex, but to whom one does not wish to imply any significant degree of commitment. *Usage: "Hey, Larissa, how are you? You look great. Let me introduce you to my friend Tara."*

hammer, *n.* A carpenter's tool consisting of a wooden or metal handle with a weighted metal end, used for driving nails.

homosexual, *n.* A person attracted to members of his or her own sex. *(Note: The ADA UDR&B has been compiled from a detailed statistical survey of heterosexual mores. It is to be used by nonheterosexuals for entertainment purposes only.)*

hot date, *n.* Any date in which intercourse is imminently anticipated.

impotence, *n.* A state of persistent and undesired nonturgidity in the penis.

lean-in, *n.* The moment in early dating at which a male attempts to kiss his potential dating partner.

lover, *n.* Someone with whom one is having intercourse on a fairly regular basis, but to whom one cannot apply a less risible term, such as "boyfriend," "girlfriend," "husband," or "wife." For this reason the term often connotes homosexuality.

MAD, *n.* See "Mutually Agreed State of Dating."

marriage, *n.* A state of permanent, legally sanctioned romantic obligation. *NB: Upon entering a condition of marriage, a person is no longer bound by the conventions outlined in this book. (Note: For further information, consult the laws of the state within which you reside, or look under "Counselors" in the yellow pages.)*

moan, *v.* To complain in an unwarranted manner, especially in an attempt to create a foul mood in others so that it will match the foul mood that one feels oneself. Cf. "bitch," "rag."

mutual, *adj.* Occurring reciprocally or by joint assent. *Usage note: Certain breakers or breakees, upon being asked who initiated the termination of their relationship, will often reply, "It was mutual." This can be taken as a sign either of guilt on the part of the breaker, or shame on the part of the breakee. Breakups are almost never, in fact, mutual.*

Mutually Agreed State of Dating, *n.* The period of time, generally occupying the bulk of a nonmarried heterosexual dating relationship, after a couple has agreed not to date any other parties, and before they have broken up, died, or gotten engaged. Abbreviated as "MAD," for no readily discernible reason.

obligation, *n.* A thing which one does not want to do, but which one must do in order to avoid earning the enmity of a person, persons, or all society. Cf. "compliant."

orgasm, *n.* The moment of intense pleasure accompanying the final moments of intercourse, regarded by many scientists and philoso-

---

Snap Rap: Obligation

Gather a group of friends together and discuss the following questions:

For men:
- Which is a worse obligation, driving your mother to the airport or having brunch with a bunch of your girlfriend's male friends?
- Has a woman ever cornered you into so many obligations that it got to the point where you just hated the sight of her face?
- Can masturbation ever be an obligation? Why not?

For women:
- Do you think your boyfriend appreciates the things you do for him?
- Do you think men have a hard time with the concept of obligation? Why?
- Have you ever made your boyfriend do something, like put on a coat and tie before dinner, just to see if he would do it? Did you succeed? How did that make you feel?

phers as the sole advantage of two-gender biology. Generally followed in the male by sleep and in the female by irritation.

POP, *n.* See "Pursuit-of-Options Period."

potential dating partner, *n.* A person of the opposite sex to whom one is not related, and with whom one might share a romantic relationship.

psycho, *n.* 1. A real or potential dating partner who has been known to be severely noncompliant in their dating behavior, to such an extent that their actions can only be understood through reference to the principals of abnormal psychology. Cf. "Rogue Dater." *Usage: "Dude, I know she's hot, and from what I heard she's got both her nipples pierced. But, dude, she burned down her last boyfriend's house because she found a Victoria's Secret catalogue in his mailbox. She's a complete and total psycho."* 2. An ex-girlfriend.

Pursuit-of-Options Period, *n.* An early stage in the courtship process in which a man and a woman meet from time to time for the purpose of exploring a mutual romantic potentiality, without having agreed not to pursue other potentialities with other parties. *(Note: See* UDR&B *Sec. IV, "Early Courtship.")*

rag, *v.* To complain in an unwarranted manner, especially about things that no one else can perceive as problematic, because one is undergoing one's menses. Cf. "bitch," "moan."

red-blooded, *adj.* Heterosexual.

Rogue Dater, *n.* A real or potential dating partner who has been frequently, and without cause, nonconcompliant in their dating behavior. Cf. "psycho." *IMPORTANT: If you have had contact with a Rogue Dater or a psycho, do not attempt to apprehend or punish them. Contact the American Dating Association Compliance Division so that swift action can be taken. For a list of Rogue Daters in your area, check the Rogue Dater Registry at www.americandating.org.*

Pop Quiz:
Match the complaint with its proper description.

Complaint:

1. "I don't know why we had to go eat Italian, I'm not even in the mood for Italian. Well, I know I said I was in the mood for Italian in the car, but that was five minutes ago."

2. "What do you mean, you pulled the shower curtain all the way closed? How the hell do you think the toilet paper roll got soaking wet? Do you think it's magic? Do you think it's fucking magic?"

3. "What is that supposed to mean, I look like Cindy Crawford in this dress? Do you think Cindy Crawford is attractive?"

4. "Fine. No, that's fine. You want to watch the Packers instead of Lifetime, that's fine. We'll do what you want. No, no. I'm not sulking. I'm not. We'll watch your little show."

5. "You have betrayed me. Now I must kill you."

Description:

a. Moaning
b. Bitching
c. Ragging

Answers: 1. a, moaning 2. b, bitching 3. c, ragging 4. a, moaning 5. Trick question—not a complaint, but a death threat.

romance, *n.* 1. [lit.] A fantastic tale. 2. A state or condition characterized by togetherness, intimacy, and the imminent commencement of sexual relations.

romantic, *adj.* 1. Inclined toward feelings and expressions of devotion and togetherness. 2. Involving sexual activity or the potential for sexual activity. 3. Atmospherically conducive to the initiation of inter-course. *Examples: 1. Flowers! My goodness, Ernest, you're so romantic. 2. Is Bob happy just being a good friend of yours, or are his intentions romantic? 3. Gosh, Tyrone, this fireplace and bearskin rug sure are romantic! Usage note: Sense 1 is only ever applied toward men, as, unlike women, this tendency is deemed re-markable when displayed by one.*

rumor, *n.* An unsourced story of doubtful veracity; generally, the first clue one has that one's partner may be noncompliant.

semen, *n.* The watery, proteinaceous ejaculate accompanying the male orgasm. *Usage note: The term "semen" is rarely used colloquially, but is preferred in public media and social settings.*

sex, *n.* Any activity which results in an orgasm, or which has the po-tential for resulting in an orgasm in a healthy adult human being. Also: sexual relations, sexual intercourse, intercourse. *Example: Martin LaRue bragged to his friends that he had "gotten laid" on his first date with Vicky Manhem. Subsequent investigation revealed that he had ejaculated while slow dancing, through no direct encouragement of his date. An ADA Arbitration Panel held that LaRue was in violation, since slow dancing in itself is not deemed a suf-ficient cause of orgasm to qualify as sex.*

sexual behavior, *n.* A class of human activity characterized by direct physical stimulation of another person's body with the aim of increas-ing erotic arousal, and including extended kissing and/or deliberate and sustained contact with breasts and/or genitals.

single, *n.* 1. A person not currently bound by the strictures of matri-mony. See "marriage." 2. A person not dating anyone exclusively at present. *Usage note: Though definition 1 obtains in official usage, such as DMV forms and census surveys, definition 2 is more usually signified in common parlance and will obtain for the purposes of this book. "I think you should meet Ryan. He's not single, but he's really hot, and I think he's about to break up with his girl-friend."*

Other Voices

Other respected quasi-governmental authorities have established some-what different criteria. For example, the following definition is contained within the Starr Report: "A person engages in 'sexual relations' when the person knowingly engages in or causes . . . contact with the genitalia, anus, groin, breast, inner thigh, or buttocks of any person with an intent to arouse or gratify the sexual desire of any person. . . . 'Contact' means intentional touching, either directly or through clothing."

Source: Independent Counsel's Report to the United States House of Representatives, Washington, D.C., 1998.

terminate, v. To end a relationship. *Usage note: "Terminate," though it can be used to refer to the ending of any relationship, is most commonly used to refer to the act of ending a relationship between two people who are not yet technically dating. (Note: See* UDR&B *Sec. IV.C.ii.b.) See also "break up."*

Section II:
Meeting

OVERVIEW: *The first meeting is where it all begins—the initial rush of excitement, the trading of glances, the terrifying and exhilarating first approach. Everything is possible, and almost nothing is known. From this tiny seed the oak of a truly great relationship can grow—or the fast-spun fantasies of romantic bliss can quickly melt into impossibility.*

Even though two potential partners are just strangers when they first meet, that doesn't mean they don't have to treat each other with a full measure of courtesy and respect. In this section we outline the standards of behavior for single people who are meeting or about to meet.

A. **Identification of Potential Dating Partners**
  ### i. **Eligibility**
   a. **Age.** Both parties shall be of age of consent mandated by the laws of their state of residence, and if above the age of seventy-five, shall have obtained written permission from their physicians verifying their fitness to engage in sexual intercourse.

   b. **Sexual orientation.** Both parties shall be heterosexual. *(Note: If either of the parties does not self-identify as heterosexual, his or her behavior is not governed by this edition of the* Universal Dating Regulations & Bylaws. *Readers of other sexual identities should refer to a sister publication, the ADA's* Gay, Lesbian, Bisexual and Transgendered Dating Regulations & Bylaws.*)*

   c. **Marital status.** Neither party shall currently be married to

WARNING

The president of the American Dating Association has determined that entering into a relationship with a noneligible person can be injurious to physical and mental health.

any other party. Parties who are separated from their current spouses shall likewise be deemed ineligible pending the results of their divorces. *(Note: Young women who are waiting for their wealthy, older married lovers to leave their wives may wish to peruse the relevant sections of the ADA's newest handbook,* Special Dating Regulations & Bylaws for Affluent Divorcés.)

d. **Substance abuse.** No full-time alcoholic, drug addict, or other chemically dependent person shall be deemed eligible to be a potential dating partner.

e. **Promiscuity.** Persons known to be extremely promiscuous shall not be deemed eligible as potential dating partners.

f. **Blood relatedness.** Parents, siblings, children, aunts, uncles, grandparents, grandchildren, and first cousins shall not be deemed eligible as potential dating partners.

g. **Age difference.** Women may seek out partners no more than four years younger than themselves. Men may seek out partners no more than y years younger than themselves, where y is defined as $(x - 13)/2$, where x represent's the man's current age.

h. **Criminality.** Unreformed criminals, who are either currently in the process of committing felonies or misdemeanors, or have recently committed felonies or misdemeanors, and are unrepentant about the fact, shall not be deemed eligible as potential dating partners.

i. **Occupation, class, and income level.** Occupation, class, and income level shall not be deemed grounds for ineligibility as a potential dating partner, with the following exceptions:

1. Movie actors
2. Strippers
3. Rock 'n' roll drummers
4. Casino developers
5. Hermits
6. Ordained Roman Catholic priests or nuns
7. Prostitutes
8. Personal injury attorneys
9. Drug dealers
10. Men who stand on street corners whistling at women
11. Incarcerated felons
12. Rogue cops

(Note: However, see UDR&B *Sec. II.B.iii.a.3, "Disclosure, Position.")*

j. **Collegiality**

1. Business colleagues, coworkers, and associates separated by more than two grades of employment shall not be deemed eligible as potential dating partners.

2. Persons shall not date or attempt to date anyone in their immediate employ or in their chain of command.

k. **Race and ethnicity.** Racial background, ethnicity, or coloration shall not be grounds for judging a potential dating partner ineligible. However, both parties must be able to understand no fewer than twenty (20) words of some mutually comprehended language.

**Dating Haiku
"On the Uptown
Number Six"**

Clack of subway wheels
Brown eyes caress a poem
Above my wool hat

—G. Laurencia Bigelow,
Buried Things, Cryptonom Press,
New York, 1983

l. **Reputation.** A bad reputation shall not be deemed grounds for ineligibility, unless it can be determined to a high degree of probability that the rumors are true. *(Note: See UDR&B Secs. II.A.i.d, e, and h, above.)*

m. **Incompetence**

    1. A person physically incapable, e.g., through lack of genitalia, of conducting a sexual relationship shall not be deemed eligible as a potential dating partner.

2. A person mentally incapable of conducting a sexual relationship, e.g., because in a coma, shall not be deemed eligible as a potential dating partner.

n. **Commonality of interests.** Prospective dating partners shall share at least one hobby, interest, or topic of enthusiasm; or, if they do not share at least one hobby, interest, or topic of enthusiasm, shall exhibit and maintain a zealous sexual appetite for one another.

o. **Attractiveness.** Unattractive people shall not attempt to date people markedly more attractive than themselves, and vice versa. Among the factors which affect the subjective assessment of attractiveness:

    1. Beauty/handsomeness

    2. Physical condition

    3. Intelligence

    4. Financial means

    5. Fame, celebrity, or renown

    6. Demeanor

(Note: An excess of one attribute may compensate for a deficit in another, but not generally in a linear fashion. See Fig. II.1.)

p. **Horoscope.** Neither party's sign of the zodiac shall be held against them in determining whether or not they are acceptable

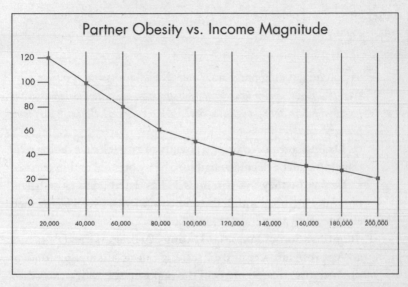

Fig. II.1. Partner Obesity vs. Income Magnitude. There are many components of attractiveness; it is rare that two members of a dating couple should exhibit an equal share of all or, indeed, any of them. A deficit in one area is generally made up for by a surplus in another, and vice versa. Above, data plotted by standard regression analysis for 2,000 American couples surveyed between 1997 and 1999. On the y-axis, the average number of pounds the female partner is overweight, plotted against the yearly income of her male partner on the x-axis. In general terms, a poor man's girlfriend is very fat, while a rich man's girlfriend is thin and attractive. *Source: ADA Multivariate Analysis Yearbook 2000.*

Rule of Thumb

Say you're standing in a bar and an attractive person of the opposite sex asks whether you're single. Are you? If in doubt, apply the physical presence test: If your partner were standing next to you, what would your answer be?

as potential dating partners. *(Note: Single men should be aware, however, that many women consider the horoscope an important tool in assessing potential future dating partners. See* UDR&B *Sec. II.B.iii.c, "Acceptable prevarication.")*

q. **Dating status.** No person already in an exclusive dating relationship shall be deemed eligible to be a potential dating partner.

r. **Dating history.** No person who has dated one's close friend or family member within the past two (2) years shall be deemed eligible to be a potential dating partner.

ii. **Identification of Potential Dating Partners–Direct**

a. **Appropriate venues.** In seeking out or attempting to identify heterosexual members of the opposite sex with whom they might hope to engage in a future dating relationship, persons shall understand that their efforts will most likely be rewarded in an environment conducive to and supportive of such an endeavor, including but not limited to

1. Parties
2. Work/business
3. Picnics
4. Church or church socials
5. Sports and other leisure activities involving common interest

WARNING

Particular care should be exercised when dating or attempting to date next-door neighbors, colleagues who work in close proximity, or any other persons who may be difficult to avoid should worse come to worst.

      6. Gym or health club

      7. Apartment buildings, condominiums, and other multiunit dwellings

      8. Laundromats

b. **Acceptable venues.** In seeking out or attempting to identify heterosexual members of the opposite sex with whom they might hope to engage in a future dating relationship, persons shall understand that their efforts may plausibly be expected to be rewarded in certain environments conducive to such endeavors, but that certain drawbacks, including a predilection for sexual predation, may undermine chances for long-term dating success.

      1. Bars *(note: for exceptions, see* UDR&B *II.A.ii.c.9)*

      2. Nightclubs

      3. Conventions *(note: for exceptions, see* UDR&B *II.A.ii.c.13)*

      4. Government offices

c. **Inappropriate venues.** Potential dating partners shall not be sought out in inappropriate venues, and any relationship that might ensue would be deemed ipso facto noncompliant. Such venues include but are not limited to

      1. Cult compounds

      2. Dungeon-style sex clubs

      3. All other varieties of sex clubs

Dating Tip

Don't enter a relationship hoping to change someone.

    4. On the street

    5. On the subway

    6. Inside a booth at a strip club

    7. In prison

    8. While parked at stop lights

    9. Bars where "ladies drink free"

    10. At home

    11. Livestock farms

    12. Right wing militia/white supremacist rallies

    13. Pornography, "Magic: The Gathering," or actuarial conventions

    14. Monasteries or nunneries

    15. AA or other twelve-step recovery programs

d. **Enlisting third-party aid.** Persons seeking a dating relationship may ask friends, neighbors, colleagues, relatives, and other acquaintances to arrange ostensibly agenda-free social occasions such as dinner parties, after-work drinks, and so forth with available single persons of the opposite sex, provided that the person seeking companionship

    1. Understands that the true motive for the occasion will have also been made clear to the other involved person or persons

    2. Will strive to maintain the ostensible agenda-free status of the occasion, so as to minimize mutual embarrassment

    3. Will at least make an attempt to get along with the other

invitees, and to appreciate their attractive sides, rather than reject them out of hand

4. Will make every effort to return the favor if and when the need should arise

e. **Bedding friends.** Persons shall be entitled to freely pursue amorous intentions regarding previously platonic friends of the opposite sex, provided there is no compelling reason for them not to. Among such compelling reasons:

1. Person has tried before and been unambiguously rejected.

2. Person has tried before, been successful, and realized that it was a big mistake.

3. Friend is only rendered temporarily attractive by one's own drunkenness.

4. Friend is disqualified by any of the reasons enumerated in *UDR&B* Sec. II.A.i, above.

iii. **Identification of Potential Dating Partners—Indirect**

a. **Blind date**

1. Having asked a friend or acquaintance to set up a blind date for them, a person shall afterward sincerely thank said friend or acquaintance for his or her trouble, and not complain that the companion on said date was weird, scary, gay, politically appalling, ill-mannered, or ugly, or that said companion smelled bad, made inappropriate advances, or made insufficient advances, even if any such claims might be true.

2. A person, asked by a single friend or acquaintance to set him or her up on a blind date, shall either refuse or seek to set up said blind date with someone whom said friend or acquaintance will most likely not find repulsive.

3. Upon arranging to meet a potential dating partner on a

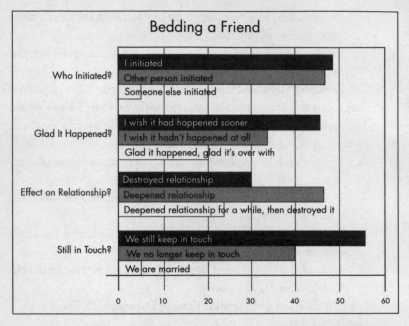

Fig. II.2. Psychological Aftermath of Sexual Relations Between Previously Platonic Friends. One thousand single heterosexual Americans between the ages of twenty-four and thirty-six who identified themselves as having slept with a formerly platonic friend within the previous sixty months were asked the following four questions: Who initiated the sexual interlude? Are you glad that the sexual interlude occurred? What effect did the sexual interlude have on your subsequent relationship? And, Do you still maintain any sort of relationship with said sexual partner? The results indicate that, for a significant number of people, having sex with a friend can have significant positive ramifications in the long as well as the short term. *Source: ADA Supplementary Third Quarter Multi-Longitudinal Survey,* December 1998.

blind date, a person shall be cognizant of the fact that, unlike most first dates, this one will take place without any evidence of mutual attraction, and will therefore willfully restrain their most eccentric behaviors or character traits, including chewing with an open mouth, the compulsive telling of dirty jokes, lengthy descriptions of arcane hobbies, and the vehement exposition of fringe political views.

4. Both parties shall understand that chances of either one finding the other companionable are slim, and thus any ex-

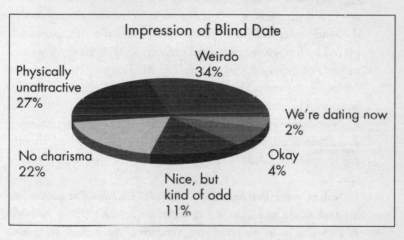

Fig. II.3. Subjective Perception of Third-Party-Arranged Potential Dating Subjects. Fifteen hundred American women between the ages of eighteen and twenty-five who had been on a blind date within the last three months were surveyed as to their subjective opinion of their most recent blind date. The most common assessments were "weirdo," with 34 percent, and "physically unattractive," with 27 percent. *Source:* Kelly, G., and Hansen, H., "An Exogenous Interpolation of Biogrammatic Data Points," *Journal of Human Relationship and Self-Esteem Research,* Vol. 234.

cuse tendered to terminate the occasion shall be immediately accepted and acted upon without further question.

5. In the unlikely event that both parties find the other's company enjoyable, the occasion shall be understood to constitute a first date, and hence will fall under the jurisdiction of the *UDR&B* Sec. III, "First Date."

b. **Dating services.** If one has met one's partner through a matchmaking or dating service, and one's partner wishes that fact to remain a secret, one shall not disclose it to any third parties.

c. **Television dating game shows.** Single heterosexuals shall not enroll themselves as contestants on television dating shows.

d. **Mail-order brides.** Persons who respond to magazine ads placed by foreign women shall only do so with an eye to matrimony, not merely dating. *(Note: The ADA suggests that persons embarking on this course should consult an immigration attorney licensed to practice in their state of residence.)*

e. **Numbers written on walls.** No one shall call any number found scrawled, scratched, inscribed, affixed, attached, or otherwise posted inside a public lavatory or any other public space.

f. **Yellow page listings.** *(Note: The ADA advises that women who list their names and photographs under the heading "Escort Services" in the yellow pages are prostitutes. Commercial transactions are against the laws of most states and are not sanctioned by the American Dating Association.)*

B. **Initiation of Contact**

  i. **Expression of Interest**

  a. A potential dating partner engaging in the following nonverbal activity shall justly be construed as indicating an interest in being approached:

Dating Tip

If someone makes eye contact with you for more than 1.5 seconds, either they're attracted to you or they think you're really weird looking.

1. Extended eye contact
2. Long, sultry gazes
3. An extended forefinger, slowly curling and uncurling
4. Poking the tongue in and out of the cheek

b. The following are not to be construed as expressions of interest:

1. Walking down the street in a summer dress
2. Walking down the street in any other form of clothing
3. The mere act of being female in public

ii. **Initial Introduction**

a. **In person.** A person introducing himself or herself to a stranger for the purpose of exploring the possibility of future romantic involvement shall with utmost diligence strive to

1. Avoid hackneyed or ridiculous pickup lines
2. Avoid insulting the person being approached
3. Be pleasant and complimentary, and use humor when appropriate
4. Acknowledge and extend full courtesy to all the companions of the person being approached
5. Forswear the use of hypnosis, advanced psychology, or witchcraft
6. Accept the possibility of rejection, indifference, or outright hostility with equanimity and poise

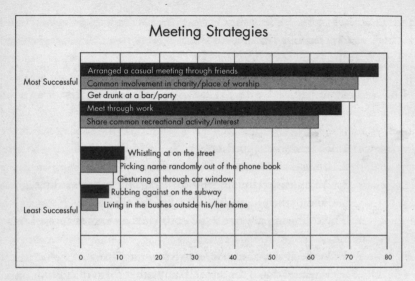

Fig. II.4. Top Strategies for Initial Interaction. Fifteen hundred single men and women in the U.S. Northeast were polled as to their favorite means of initiating contact with members of the opposite sex. Arranging to spend time with such persons at work, at church, or in social settings ranked highly. Shouting at and rubbing against strangers were deemed ineffective strategies. *Source:* Peters, J., and Brainert, D., "Changing Perceptions of Courtship Modalities," *Journal of Psychosexuality and Relationship Studies,* Vol. XVIII.

b. **Over the telephone: Cold calling.** Prospective daters shall not cold-call people they have never met, and shall be aware that Caller ID functionality is now in widespread use by the general public as well as the police.

c. **Over the Internet:** Persons with whom one has established a long and lasting rapport via chat rooms or other electronic forums may pursue more intimate, face-to-face contact. *(Note: Upon* *meeting such potential dating partners, persons shall attempt to be open-minded about said partner's appearance, mannerisms, and true gender.)*

iii. **Initial Conversation**

a. **Disclosure.** In the course of the initial conversation with a potential future dating partner, a person shall be forthright on the following subjects:

1. **Existing romantic attachments.** If a person is already in an exclusive relationship with someone else, and hence considers himself or herself unavailable, he or she should make the other person aware of this fact within the first five (5) minutes of conversation. *(Note 1: UDR&B Sec. II.B.iii.a.1 should not be taken as license to mention one's girlfriend or boyfriend in every other sentence in every conversation one has. Note 2: If one is currently dating another person but has not yet explicitly agreed that said arrangement is exclusive, one is not obligated to mention said relationship; see UDR&B Sec. V.B., "Exclusivity." See also: UDR&B Sec. II.A.i.q, "Dating status," above.)*

2. **Age.** A person may not fudge, fiddle, distort, or confabulate his or her true age, nor keep his or her age secret.

3. **Position.** A person must be forthright in revealing the nature of his or her job, including job title, description, and responsibilities. *(Note: However, see UDR&B Sec.II.B.iii.b.1, "Nondisclosure, Salary," below.)*

4. **Elective plastic surgery.** All Americans are entitled to know what their partners' actual unmodified appearance may be, and so any surgically induced changes to that appearance must be disclosed at the time of first meeting.

5. **Original gender.** If a person's birth gender is different from his or her current apparent or actual gender, that fact

ADA Case Study

In March 1987, Theodore "Bud" Sizemore began dating Ellen Eleniak, a fellow student at the University of Wisconsin. The two saw quite a bit of each other, and by late April had entered into an exclusive relationship. In the first week of May, however, he stopped calling, and Eleniak did not even lay eyes on Sizemore again until the following semester. Annoyed, she filed a Rogue Dater petition with the ADA, citing Sizemore's failure to maintain contact despite their exclusive dating status. In his defense, Sizemore argued that Eleniak had misled him contrary to the provisions of *UDR&B* Sec. II.B.iii.a.4: he had stumbled across a picture of her as a twelve-year-old and could clearly see that her nose had been much larger. In its subsequent investigation the ADA Compliance Division Review Panel discovered that the allegation was indeed true. In its ruling, the panel noted that while Eleniak had been noncompliant, Sizemore had also been noncompliant in failing to break up with Eleniak face-to-face. However, it rejected Eleniak's petition due to her own prior noncompliance, noting: "Those who wish to enjoy the benefits of sound dating practice must embody it themselves."

must be revealed to any potential dating partners within the first fifteen minutes of the initial conversation.

b. **Nondisclosure.** While a person may not lie about the following subjects in the course of an initial conversation with a potential dating partner, one is not obligated to bring them up, nor is one obligated to answer direct or indirect queries about them:

1. **Salary.** No person shall be obliged to disclose his or her salary, or the size of his or her income from any source, dur-

Stat Attack:
Are You Who You Say You Are?

Description	People who claim to be	People who really are
Harvard graduate	7 percent	0.001 percent
Movie producer	3 percent	0.000001 percent
Government agent	11 percent	0.0053 percent*
Virgins	14 percent	2 percent

*excludes postal employees

Source: Global Statistical Yearbook and Day Planner, 1999.

ing the initial conversation or at any point during a romantic relationship.

2. **Sexual history.** No person shall be obligated to reveal the extent to which his or her previous sexual history deviated from societal norms, whether from excessive frequency or infrequency, or from nonnormative modes of expression.

3. **Military service.** No person shall be obligated to discuss his or her previous military service, or lack thereof.

4. **Education.** No person shall be obligated to explain or enumerate his or her academic failings or inability to obtain a degree, nor shall a person be required to explain his or her choice of an ostensibly useless college major, as for instance Art History.

c. **Acceptable prevarication.** If compelled by social exigency, a person may with justification make misleading statements about

1. His or her zodiac sign
2. His or her true feelings about pets
3. His or her enthusiasm for professional sports

C. Assessment

Upon the completion of the introductory conversation, a person's conduct shall reflect whether or not he or she desires further contact.

i. **Further Contact Is Desired.** If a person desires further contact, or is not yet able to entirely rule out the possibility of such a desire in the future, he or she shall behave in accordance with his or her gender.

a. **Male.** A male desiring further contact shall ask for the female's telephone number, with the following provisos:

1. If for some reason he prefers not to use the telephone, he may request the woman's email address.

2. If the initial conversation lasts not less than twenty (20) minutes, and if the man feels that a truly remarkable bond has formed between himself and the potential dating partner, then he may instead suggest that the couple immediately spend more time together. Intermediate steps may then be skipped. *(Note: See* UDR&B *Sec. III, "First Date.")*

b. **Female.** A female desiring further contact may not ask for the male's phone number, but may express her interest in any of the following ways:

1. Hinting at interest in future events, including upcoming movies, parties, concerts, sporting events, and other occasions of presumable mutual interest.

2. Hinting at some future opening in her social calendar. *Example: "I was supposed to go the beach Saturday but my flaky roommate bagged on me."*

3. Mentioning some extant location, building, site, store, or place of presumed mutual interest. *Example: "Have you seen the Getty yet?"*

ii. **No Further Contact Is Desired.** If, upon completing a conversation of sufficient duration to accurately assess his or her likely future level of interest in a potential dating partner, a person becomes convinced that he or she desires no further contact, he or she shall extricate himself or herself from the conversation with as little emotional disruption as possible, according to his or her role as the initiator or recipient of the initial exchange.

a. **The initiator.** Upon deciding that he or she does not, contrary to initial supposition, desire further contact with the potential dating partner, the initiator may move to terminate the exchange through any of the following methods:

1. Express his or her pleasure at having met the recipient, and express a cheerful confidence that they will soon meet and renew their incipient friendship. Both parties shall understand that, the initiator having declined to request the re-

---

A Closer Look: Is it Cool to "Play It Cool"?

In recent years a common dating strategy is to "play it cool," that is, to avoid seeming too interested in a potential dating partner. For many daters, this has led to an alarming increase in the general level of ambiguity. All daters in the United States must understand that overplaying their insouciance at critical junctures such as that covered in *UDR&B* Sec. II.C.i can easily cause daters to cross the line from savvy dating to out-and-out noncompliance.

Discussion Points

After reading carefully through Section II, think about the following questions, or talk them over with a friend:

—What's the most horrible thing that ever happened to you while attempting to introduce yourself to an attractive stranger?
—Have you ever agreed to give your phone number to someone because they seemed so pathetic you didn't have the heart not to?
—Have you ever had this technique work for you?
—Do you ever think that life would be a lot simpler if we didn't have to deal with the whole issue of love, sex, and all that stuff?

cipient's phone number or otherwise express interest, future contact will be avoided.

2. Suggest that he or she has a friend, of his or her own gender, whom the recipient might like to meet.

3. Make reference to an imaginary boyfriend or girlfriend. *(Note: This strategy may only be used within the first five [5] minutes of conversation; see* UDR&B *Sec. II.B.iii.a.1.)*

b. **The recipient.** Upon discerning beyond all reasonable doubt that he or she desires no further contact with the initiator of the exchange, the recipient may move to terminate the conversation by any of the following methods:

1. Stating that it has been nice to meet the initiator, but that he or she has other things to do.

2. Refusing the initiator's request for a phone number, and

suggesting that the initiator pass along his or her own instead. Both parties shall understand that the recipient has no intention of calling the initiator, although he or she may at some future time change his or her mind if suddenly overcome with loneliness or desperation.

3. If the initiator persists in attempting to pursue further conversation, the recipient may physically flee, cry for help, or, if necessary, make threatening gestures with any available weapon such as mace or a firearm.

D. **Intimacy**

It is noncompliant to engage in physical intimacy or romantic passion with someone without first going on a date with him or her. *(Note: Examples of noncompliant pre-date intimacy include drunken hooking-up at a party, picking up strangers in bars, and fondling coworkers in the stairwell.)*

Section III:
First Date

OVERVIEW: *The first date is the most perilous, danger-fraught period of a nascent relationship. Every gesture, word, and action is laden with a host of clues as to a person's personality and intentions. Given the high stakes and emotionally charged atmosphere, it can be difficult to achieve that all-important state of ease and relaxation. But remember: If two people are meant to be together, their mutual attraction will overcome any minor hurdles.*

A. Arranging of First Date

i. Responsibility

a. Regardless of who initiated contact in the first place, it is the man's responsibility to contact the woman next, with the following exceptions:

> 1. The man is incapacitated, physically handicapped, heavily medicated, or in some other way unable to pick up a telephone.
>
> 2. The woman is substantially richer, more famous, or in any other way intimidatingly more put together than the man.

b. Acceptable modes for contact include the telephone and email.

c. If, having called the telephone number provided to him by the woman, the man reaches a suicide crisis hotline, a pizza delivery restaurant, or a nonworking number, it is his responsibility to recognize that his companionship is not desired, and he will make no further efforts to pursue a relationship with the woman in question.

d. If, after a man calls a woman on the telephone, she says, "Oh, I'm on the other line, give me your number, I'll call you right back," and then never does, the man shall understand that his attentions are not desired, and he will make no further attempts to pursue his romantic interest.

ii. **Interval Before Subsequent Contact**

a. If a man is attracted to a woman, and desires to pursue her as a potential dating partner, he must contact her within the following time frame:

1. He may contact her no sooner than two (2) days after their initial introduction.

2. He must contact her no later than five (5) days after their initial introduction.

b. If a man is in no way attracted to a woman, and is quite certain that he has no desire to engage in a romantic relationship with her at the current time or at any time in the future, he must contact her within the following time frame:

1. He may contact her whenever he wishes, but he must make clear that he has no intention of ever dating her, and that his desire is strictly for a platonic friendship or business relationship.

2. He is free to never contact her again, without receiving any bitching, moaning, or ragging from any mutual friends he may happen to share with the woman in question.

iii. **Incubation Period.** The period subsequent to an initial meeting and prior to a first date shall be termed the "incubation period."

a. If a man is insufficiently confident of his charm and/or appeal with regards to the woman in question, he may engage in one or more rounds of conversation on the telephone or exchanges of email during the incubation period before requesting a first date.

b. Having reached a woman over the telephone or by email, a man shall make every effort to engage her attention in a relaxed, friendly, nonpretentious manner.

c. Having sent an email or made a telephone call, a man may not again contact the woman until said email or phone call has been returned.

d. A man may send no more than five (5) emails before he must call and conduct a live conversation over the telephone.

e. The incubation period shall last no longer than four (4) weeks except under powerfully extenuating circumstances, e.g., one or both parties is forced to leave the country.

iv. **Request for a Date**

a. In asking the woman out on a date, he will balance the perceived level of intimacy achieved so far with the intimacy level

Stat Attack

Every 4.2 seconds, on average, somewhere in the United States a single heterosexual is experiencing an orgasm.

Source: 1999 ADA Factbook.

of the day for which he is suggesting they meet. The degree of intimacy of each day is as follows, from highest to lowest:

1. Saturday night
2. Friday night
3. Thursday night
4. Wednesday and Tuesday (tied)
5. Monday
6. Any afternoon, including lunch and/or coffee
7. Any morning, including breakfast

b. The man will not ask a woman out on a date on a Sunday night except under extraordinary circumstances, such as:

1. He will be leaving town for six months or more, and a Sunday evening is the only night on which the date can possibly be arranged.

2. He works every night of the week except Sundays, or is otherwise nonnegotiably indisposed every other night of the week.

c. The man will not propose a day and time of meeting less than twenty-four (24) hours from the current moment of conversation, nor more than seven (7) days from the current moment of conversation.

d. If the woman says that she is not free at the time which he proposes for the date, the man shall recognize that his request for a date has been turned down, and will press the issue no further. Exceptions:

1. The woman immediately proposes an alternative date or time.

2. The woman offers a convincing reason why the date is not possible (e.g., she will be out of the country or undergo-

A Closer Look:
Calling to Make a First Date

When calling to arrange for a first date, what should I do if the woman isn't there? Should I leave a message?

Generally, no. There exists in our society a powerful moral force which prevents women from calling men, even if it is to return a previous call. Therefore, you should seriously try to get her on the phone.

This usually isn't a problem if you have her work number, since most people's jobs require them to be easily reachable. If you have only her home number, try to call her at a time when she's likely to be home, such as shortly after she gets off work but before she might leave home again for a dinner engagement (the period from 6:30 P.M. to 7:30 P.M. is known as the "golden hour" for this purpose). Ten o'clock to 11 P.M. can also be a good bet, unless you know she's an early riser. Sunday at 11 A.M. is also a high-probability time, but *not if you only met her the previous Friday or Saturday night.*

If you get her answering machine, hang up. Try again later. Make at least three attempts to get her live on the phone. (In areas which offer Caller ID service, make sure to dial *67 before you dial. When you do reach her, you want her to assume you're calling for the first time.)

If you still haven't reached her after three attempts, then go ahead and leave a message. She may be screening her calls, or she just may never be in. You have to get on with your life.

Make sure not to sound rushed or tense in your message, but don't dawdle. Go on for twenty-five to forty-five seconds, reminding her of where you talked, and pleasantly extending some conversation you had. Then leave your number, and get off.

I left a message, and she hasn't called back. Should I try again?

No. She got your message. There's only one reason why she hasn't called you back: She doesn't want to go on a date with you.

But I left the message with a shiftless/vindictive/non-native-English-speaking roommate. Or, I left it on her machine, but she warned me that sometimes her machine doesn't work.

There's always a chance—a small chance, but greatly magnified by desperation—that she really was waiting for your call, but that somehow the message got lost in transit. But you know what? You still shouldn't call.

But she really, really seemed to like me.

She probably did. But then she had a chance to think it over.

But I've seen movies, or heard stories from friends, in which a guy won a girl over through persistence.

Yeah, but they were friends, not strangers who had only met once. Nobody loves a stalker.

ing surgery) and immediately suggests a time period during which she will be free.

v. **Predate Contact**
   a. If either party so desires, he or she may suggest that a final determination as to the time and/or place of their meeting will be made at a future point, such as the morning of the date in question. ·

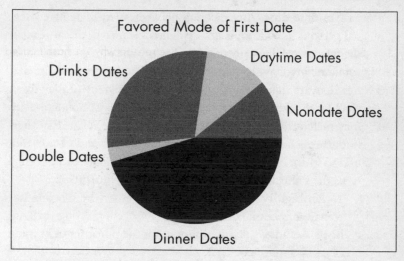

Fig. III.1. Favored Mode of First Date. Five hundred single persons between the ages of nineteen and twenty-nine were polled by telephone and asked what was their favored form of first date. A large plurality, 46 percent, said that they favored the dinner date, while only a very small minority (<5 percent) indicated that their favored mode was the double date. The data would tend to support the hypothesis that most single heterosexuals prefer more intimate forms of dating to those with less intensive courtship interaction. *Source:* Gray, J., *Mars and Venus Get in a Rocket Ship and Fly to the Moon,* 2000.

> b. Whichever party is charged with calling to verify the arrangements of said date shall not fail to do so.
>
> c. Neither party shall call the other prior to the agreed meeting time, unless significant unexpected developments necessitate the rearrangement or cancellation of the date.
>
> vi. **Mode of Date.** The type of date to be arranged shall be in concordance with the general level of intimacy sought. In increasing level of intimacy, these are

a. **Nondate date.** Any meeting between two single heterosexual persons in which it is not evidently clear to both parties that the purpose of their meeting is to further the pursuit of potential romantic involvement, and yet at which at least one of the parties is aware that the potential for such involvement may exist, shall be considered a nondate date. Examples of nondate dates may include after-work dinners with colleagues, Saturday afternoon brunches with clients, a drink with a friend of a friend, and so forth. Nondate dates shall be treated under these regulations the same as other dates, with the following provisos:

1. **Ambiguity.** Uncertainty as to whether the meeting has romantic potential or is simply an innocent meeting shall not be deliberately cultivated simply for the purposes of keeping one's options open. *(Note: However, ambiguity may be cultivated to avoid an oppressive feeling of awkwardness.)*

2. **Unfamiliarity.** Nondate dates may be made without the parties ever having previously met, based on mutual acquaintance, common business interests, and so forth.

3. **Trappings.** Neither party may violate the ambiguity of the nondate date with any trappings of overt dateness, such as flowers, candles, soft music, romantic words, caresses, and the like.

4. **Convertibility.** If, at any time in the course of the nondate date, either party expresses a wish for romantic attachment, or in any other way violates the ambiguity of the occasion, the nondate date shall convert to an overt date, to be classified according to the descriptions that follow. *Example: If Bob and Laura are colleagues having an ostensibly platonic after-work dinner together, and Bob asks Laura to go home with him,*

the occasion shall immediately be reclassified as a dinner date according to the provisions of UDR&B *Sec. III.A.vi.e, below.*

b. **Daytime dates.** Defined as any date which begins no later than half an hour before sunset, and concludes no later than half an hour after sunset, daytime dates are the least intimate of all overt dates. Parties undertaking to meet for a daytime date shall understand that the likelihood of physical romantic activity is low. Such dates may include

1. Coffee
2. Lunch
3. A matinee movie
4. Walk in the park

(Note: If both parties work the night shift, and/or have recently arrived at their current location from a spot on the other side of the globe where the time zone is at least ten hours different, then the term "daytime dates" shall be understood to apply to dates which take place during the nighttime, and vice versa.)

c. **Drinks dates.** Regarded as a moderate first date for persons uncertain about their romantic prospects or desires, drinks dates are characterized by maximum flexibility and are defined as any date which exhibits all of the following characteristics:

1. **Timing.** At least some significant portion of the drinks date must take place later than a half hour after sunset.

2. **Consumption.** In the course of the date, both parties shall have an opportunity to consume some form of light food and/or beverage, the social norm being alcoholic beverages. This consumption may or may not be accompanied by some form of entertainment, such as jukebox music, gallery paintings, or a baseball game on television.

Stat Attack:
Let's Get Together

When calling to arrange a date, men receive a favorable response 64 percent of the time when they propose a specific and timely activity, such as attending a gallery opening or local street fair. When the proposal was made in vague terms of "coming out for a drink," it met with a favorable response only 43 percent of the time.

Source: Hey, There, Good Lookin': A Multi-Phasic Double-Blind Counterweighted Social Perceptions Survey of American Males 24–26 Years of Age, R. Fury, ed., ADA Publishing House, New York, 1998.

     3. **Convertibility.** If, in the course of the drinks date, both parties become aware that they desire to spend more time together, they must have the option to proceed at that point to having dinner together, at which point the drinks date will convert to a dinner date. *(Note: See* UDR&B *Sec. III.A.vi.e.)*

  d. **Double dates.** A double date, namely a date which exhibits all the properties of a dinner date *(note: see* UDR&B *Sec. III.A.vi.e)* but is conducted in the company of another couple, may be arranged if either party is uncomfortable with the idea of spending a good deal of potentially intimate time with the other. *(Note: If the double date does not involve dinner, it is not technically a date at all, but merely a group of friends spending time together.)*

  e. **Dinner dates.** The most intimate of all first dates, the dinner date is also the most popular *(note: see Fig. III.1),* especially among singles with a keen interest in "closing." *(Note: See* UDR&B *Sec. I, "close.")* The defining characteristics of a dinner date are as follows:

1. The sharing of the evening meal, usually but not necessarily preceded, accompanied, and followed with the imbibing of alcoholic beverages.

2. Other entertainment preceding or following the meal, such as a movie, concert, dancing, or karaoke, are frequent but not required components of the dinner date.

3. The man must personally pay for the dinner. *(Note: See* UDR&B *Sec. I, "Dutch treat." Should a man refuse to pay the entirety of the meal bill, or attempt to charge said bill to his corporate expense account, the date shall no longer be considered a dinner date, but shall revert to the status of nondate date. See* UDR&B *Sec. III.A.vi.a.)*

4. The man shall pay for all ancillary entertainment expenses, including ticket fees, taxes, tips, and miscellaneous charges.

5. The woman shall not order the most expensive thing on the menu, unless the most expensive item on the menu is less than ten dollars, or if the man has boasted within the previous hour about how wealthy he is.

6. The man shall retain responsibility for ordering the wine, if any.

7. The man shall not pressure the woman to order the burger, or to forego an appetizer, drinks, or dessert.

8. Both parties shall understand that the expense of the meal shall not in any way necessitate a commensurate display of affection on the part of the woman later in the date.

B. **Behavior**

i. **Congeniality.** In the course of a first date, each party shall endeavor to maintain a congenial, warm, and kind atmosphere, free from affectation or malicious scheming.

a. **Avoidance of affectation.** Both parties shall eschew affectation, and instead attempt to conduct themselves in a manner as closely fitting with their own actual personality as is possible.

1. Neither party shall quote philosophers, authors, poets, or other learned persons whose work they have never read.

2. Neither party shall boast unnecessarily of their education, income, upbringing, breeding, or personal possessions.

3. Neither party shall speak French, under any pretext whatsoever.

b. **Attentiveness.** Each person shall endeavor to honor the other with the greater part of his or her attention.

1. Neither person shall forget the other person's name.

2. Neither person shall ask the same question (such as where he or she grew up, what his or her astrological sign is, how many siblings he or she has, whether he or she has ever broken his or her leg skiing, etc.) more than twice.

3. Neither party shall stare at, gawk at, or ogle any person of the opposite sex, other than the person they are on the date with.

c. **Disposition.** Each party shall strive to maintain a pleasant disposition. *(Note: See also* UDR&B *Sec. III.B.v.)*

1. Neither party shall bark at, insult, or threaten waitstaff.

2. Neither party shall become obnoxiously drunk.

3. Neither party shall engage in, or threaten to engage in, violence with any third party.

4. Neither party shall attempt to sell insurance to the other.

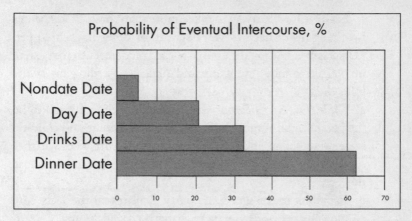

Fig. III.2. Probability of Sexual Congress As a Function of Date Modality. One thousand single men between the ages of twenty-five and thirty-five were polled as to what type of first date they had last been on, and whether or not they had succeeded in achieving sexual congress with their partner. Of those who reported that their previous first date had been a dinner date, 63 percent indicated that they had achieved sexual congress. A much smaller proportion, 32 percent, of men who had been on a drinks date had managed to achieve sexual relations. While hardly surprising, these data may be problematic in that they rely on self-reporting by young males, a notoriously unreliable group, particularly on matters of sexual self-analysis. *Source: Guy* magazine, "Bonk-a-Palooza," January 2000.

ii. **Discretion.** In the course of a first date, each party shall scrupulously maintain an air of discretion regarding the following topics:

a. **Exes.** Neither party shall discuss, complain about, or reminisce over any ex-girlfriend or ex-boyfriend, unless specifically and directly asked to do so.

b. **Salary.** Neither party shall inquire about the other's level of remuneration, nor shall they in any way make known their own.

   c. **Pets.** Neither party shall relate more than three (3) anecdotes involving his or her beloved dog, cat, or other household pet.

iii. **Disclosure.** During the course of the first date, each party shall be obliged to fully reveal any and all facts regarding any of the following:

a. **Children.** Any person who knows himself or herself to be the parent of an extant child or children, whether said children were produced in or out of wedlock, and regardless of whether or not he or she has ever met said children, shall fully disclose the fact.

b. **Previous marriage.** Each party shall reveal the facts concerning any previous marriage or marriages, including

   1. The causes and mode of dissolution, whether divorce, annulment, or death

   2. The current whereabouts of any extant ex-wives or ex-husbands

c. **Felony convictions.** Each party shall disclose any felony convictions, regardless of whether the

   1. Crime was violent or white-collar

   2. Crime was a federal or state offense

   3. Sentence was served or commuted

   4. Conviction was arrived at by plea bargain or jury verdict

d. **Gang membership.** Each party shall fully disclose any current or previous membership in illegal gangs, including

   1. Prison gangs

   2. Street gangs

   3. Mafia, Italian

   4. Mafia, Colombian

   5. Mafia, Russian

   6. Mafia, Chechen

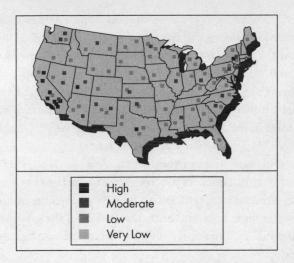

Fig. III.3. Felonious Daters. A sample-normalized demographical distribution map of felons as a percentage of single adult heterosexual population, by county. Areas in black indicate that more than 5 percent of all single adult heterosexuals have done time for a conviction of felony grade or higher. Areas in light gray indicate that fewer than 1 percent of the single adult heterosexuals are convicted felons. Notice that a felon-free band runs from North Dakota south to the Texas panhandle. *Source: Criminology and Dating: A Field Study Handbook, ADA Publishing Syndicate, 1999.*

e. **Severe medical conditions.** A person shall fully disclose any potentially life-threatening medical conditions which might cause his or her incipient fatality in the course of future dating situations, including

1. Heart conditions
2. High blood pressure
3. Motorcycle ownership

f. **Ongoing or recurring mental health issues.** Any person currently undergoing treatment or therapy or receiving medication for a mental health issue of any kind, whether neurotic or psychotic, or who has received treatment, therapy, or medication at any time in the previous four (4) years, shall make this fact known to any potential future dating parties within the course of the first date. *(Note: Cf. UDR&B Sec. III.B.iv.a, "Nondisclosure, Resolved mental health issues," below.)*

g. **Ultimate noncompatibility.** Any person who becomes aware in the course of the first date that there exists the potential for ultimate long-term incompatibility based on nonnegotiable criteria must fully and immediately reveal the grounds for said potential incompatibility. Such grounds include but are not limited to

1. Perceived need to have at least three children by age thirty

2. Determination to live in Paris for at least ten years at some point in his or her life

3. Requirement that any future dating partner must profoundly love cats

4. Profound and permanent distaste for the condition of sexual monogamy

iv. **Nondisclosure.** While no person shall lie about the following subjects, neither is one obligated to bring them up, or obligated to answer direct or indirect queries about them:

a. **Resolved mental health issues.** Neither party shall be obligated to reveal or discuss mental health problems which have been fully resolved and which have not required treatment, therapy, or medication at any time within the previous four (4) years.

b. **Hobbies.** No person shall be obligated to describe his or her hobbies, particularly if they involve

1. Dungeons & Dragons
2. Society for Creative Anachronism
3. Dressing up in costumes and singing
4. *Star Trek*
5. Collectibles
6. *Star Trek* collectibles

> **Dating Haiku**
> **"The Movie"**
>
> Bucket of popcorn
> Elbows meet over armrests
> Tang of salt on lips
>
> —G. Laurencia Bigelow,
> *Moon and Moonlight,*
> Firelight Publishing,
> Seattle, 1992

c. **Internet.** No person shall be obligated to reveal

1. How many hours they spend each day on the Internet
2. The extent of their obsession with particular sites on the Internet, such as eBay
3. What the content is of the file marked "misc. stuff" buried deep inside their "personal" bookmark file

d. **Misdemeanor convictions.** No person shall be obligated to reveal misdemeanor convictions, moving violations, drunk and disorderly citations, and similar low-grade offenses, particularly if they were incurred in the offender's distant youth.

e. **Charges not brought or charges dropped.** No person shall be obligated to reveal alleged past crimes for which no charges were brought or for which no conviction was obtained.

f. **Sense of humor.** No person who has a stupid, corny, or utterly vacant sense of humor shall be obliged to reveal this fact by

1. Telling jokes
2. Singing silly songs

3. Attempting party tricks

4. Talking in funny voices, especially of beloved cartoon characters from childhood

g. **Corrective plastic surgery.** No person who has obtained plastic surgery for the purpose of correcting an injury or birth defect shall be obligated to reveal that fact on a first date.

h. **Scary family.** No person shall be obligated to reveal the existence of or details about any family members concerning whom he or she feels a deep antipathy or shame.

v. **Date-Terminating Behavior.** If either party engages in any of the following behaviors, the other party is entitled to consider him or her to be in violation of acceptable dating practice, and to consider the date effectively terminated:

a. Pursuing romantic potentialities with anyone else encountered in the course of the date, including

1. Complimenting the physique of

2. Buying a drink for

3. Asking the phone number of

4. Leaving with

b. Insulting the other person

c. Soliciting sexual intercourse without attempting to kiss the other person first

d. Masturbating in public

e. Threatening the other person with violence

f. Striking, shooting, or stabbing the other person

g. Getting into a brawl with anyone

h. Becoming so drunk that one is unable to stand up or speak clearly

i. Attempting to drive a vehicle into a crowd of pedestrians

j. Getting arrested

C. Intimacy

  i. **Baseline.** The baseline level of intimacy at the beginning of the date shall be either the Standard Stranger Intimacy Baseline (SSIB) or the Last Established Intimacy Level (LEIL), whichever is greater.

   a. **SSIB.** The Standard Stranger Intimacy Baseline is the common designated intimacy level among strangers in North America. Acceptable behaviors include

   1. Broad smile
   2. Hearty greeting
   3. Handshake, one-handed
   4. Handshake, two-handed

   b. **LEIL.** The Last Established Intimacy Level is defined simply as the degree of intimacy achieved at the most recent meeting. These are defined according to the Fujita Intimacy Scale as follows, from least to most intimate:

   1. **F1: SSIB.** The default level of intimacy, common to all strangers. *(Note: See* UDR&B *Sec. III.C.i.a, above.)*

   2. **F2: Amicable acquaintance.** The level of intimacy shared by inviduals who have met at least once and are not

---

Stat Attack

Seventy-three percent of all American men consume some form of breath mint, gum, or spray before a first kiss. Of these, 92 percent will never again use such a product in the course of an ensuing relationship.

Source: Confederation of American Breath Product Manufacturers.

disagreeably disposed toward one another. Acceptable behaviors include all above, plus hand on back, social kiss,
loose hug.

3. **F3: Friend.** The level of intimacy shared by individuals
who have established an amiable relationship. Acceptable
behaviors include all above, plus earnest hugs, cheek kiss
(contact between lip and skin of cheek).

4. **F4: Gropy friend.** The level of intimacy shared by individuals whose friendship is infused with crypto-carnal
insinuations. Acceptable behaviors include all above, plus
tight hugs, hands on back and waist, lip-on-lip contact kissing.

5. **F5: Preliminary date.** The level of intimacy shared by
individuals who have just begun dating, or who have kissed
passionately but not yet had intercourse. Acceptable behaviors include all above, plus hand-holding, French kissing,
above-the-waist groping.

6. **F6: Established date.** The level of intimacy shared by
individuals who have slept together. Acceptable behaviors
include all above, plus unlimited groping and sexual intercourse.

7. **F7: Long-term date.** The level of intimacy shared by
individuals who have been together so long that they keep
a significant proportion of their personal effects at one
another's dwellings. Acceptable behaviors include all above,
plus fetish play and the videotaping of each other having sex.

8. **F8: Moved in.** The level of intimacy shared by individuals who have been together a long time and are now cohabiting. Acceptable behaviors include all above, plus farting and
urinating in one another's presence.

A Closer Look:
The Scientific Legacy of Dr. Wayne Fujita

The story of the invention of the Fujita Intimacy Scale is all the more remarkable for being true.

Born in 1938 in San Francisco, Dr. Fujita began his professional life as a cognitive sciences researcher at the University of Texas at Austin. Investigating the ways in which intimacy levels affect cognitive mapping paradigms, Dr. Fujita was stumped by the long-standing problem of how to quantify intimacy levels so that they could be manipulated by mathematical equations.

Increasingly possessed by the subject, Dr. Fujita began to work long hours, obsessively struggling to come up with a solution. Neglecting his home life, he was abandoned by his frustrated wife. Soon after, he was evicted from his laboratory. With nowhere else to turn, Dr. Fujita moved his research to the Dew Drop Inne across town from campus. It was the only bar in Austin that would still grant him credit.

One night, while a freak outbreak of twisters scoured Austin's abandoned streets, a drunken Dr. Fujita hit upon his long-sought answer. Scribbling furiously, he committed his discovery onto the nearest available piece of paper—a disposable napkin that had been soaking up the condensation from his old-fashioned. Fujita's breakthrough: Intimacy could be scored on an absolute grade from 1 (strangers) to 10 (long-married couple). It was an achievement of earth-shattering proportions, and the scale now in use is exactly as Dr. Fujita devised it—with the addition of the letter F before each number in honor of its inventor. The napkin is currently a part of the collection of the University of Texas at Austin, and holds pride of place at the university museum.

9. **F9: Engaged.***
10. **F10: Married.***

ii. **Increasing Intimacy.** Most first dates begin at intimacy level F2 or F3 and increase to F4 or F5, though they have been recorded, in some extraordinary and very dangerous cases, going as high as F8. Regardless of the ultimate level attained, the progressive increase of intimacy shall be characterized by

a. **Orderliness.** Progression from one intimacy level to the next shall follow in a stepwise manner. A person seeking to extend the date's intimacy level will not leapfrog past intimacy mileposts, nor retreat for extended periods of time to less intimate zones than those already explored. The regions of the human body, in order from least to most intimate, are

1. Elbow, clothed
2. Knee, clothed
3. Elbow, bare
4. Knee, bare
5. Back, clothed
6. Hand, back
7. Waist, clothed
8. Hand, front
9. Hair
10. Face
11. Thigh, clothed
12. Thigh, bared
13. Breasts, clothed

---

* *Note: The American Dating Association is not chartered to offer advice on, or generate data on, intimacy levels of F9 and higher. Interested parties seeking information on postmarital intimacy should refer to the National Union of Married Persons.*

14. Genitals, clothed
15. Breasts, bared
16. Genitals, bared

b. **Atmosphere.** It shall be the obligation of the man to provide a venue suitable for the attainment of increased intimacy, such as the following:

1. Cozy restaurant
2. Movie with romantic theme
3. Dimly lit jazz bar
4. Pleasant-smelling, clean apartment with comfortable seating and an appropriate musical selection

c. **Tacit consent.** If a person touches the other person, and the other person flinches, the originator of the gesture must withdraw.

d. **Enthusiasm.** If a person touches the other person, and the other person does not react in any way, the originator may maintain the physical contact, but may not proceed into more intimate territory.

iii. **First Kiss**

a. A man may not ask for permission to kiss a woman for the first time.

b. If a man desires to kiss a woman, he must simply lean in and kiss her, provided he has

1. Gazed into her eyes
2. Touched her affectionately
3. Stopped talking

c. Unless a date has gone horribly awry, both parties may expect to kiss upon parting.

d. If a first date at no juncture contains a kiss with lip-on-lip

Fig. III.4. Preferred Scenarios for Achieving First Kiss. A group of 800 Navy pilots were queried as to their preferred venue when attempting to kiss a woman for the first time. More than a quarter responded that the car was their favorite place, while a slightly smaller percentage replied that they preferred to attempt the first kiss while strolling. Some researchers have argued that these data should be viewed skeptically, as the psychoschemata of military pilots is not generally viewed as normative. *Source:* "Hunks of the Sixth Fleet," *Department of Defense Quarterly Review,* Oct.–Dec. 1998.

contact, then both parties shall understand that the possibility of future romantic interaction will be remote.

iv. **High-Level Intimacy.** If intimacy above F5, including sexual intercourse, occurs on a first date, then both parties shall understand that the ensuing relationship will be primarily and fundamentally about sex.

D. **Subsequent Contact**

i. **Expression of Intent by the Man**

a. **Following a satisfactory date.** If after a first date a man shall have judged a woman to merit further pursuit of potential romantic interest, he shall call her no later than one week after time of initial date, and not less than 24 hours after time of initial date.

Pop Quiz

1. Bill asks Peggy out for dinner on Friday and has a so-so time. He's lonely, but not that lonely. When is the earliest he may call her?
   a. one week b. three weeks c. never

2. Phoebe has a date with Marvin on June 24. He never calls. What is the earliest date by which her friends can start giving him a hard time about it?
   a. June 25 b. July 1 c. never

3. After a wonderful evening together, Baxter drops off Susie at her home at 11 P.M. on Friday, August 17. He's so excited, he can't wait to call her. But he doesn't want to appear overeager, either. When is the latest moment he can call?

a. 3 P.M., August 18 b. 6 A.M., August 24 c. 11 P.M., August 24

Answers: 1. b 2. c 3. c

b. **Following a suboptimal date.** If after their first date a man has judged a woman to merit only marginal future potential romantic interest, he shall call her no later than six months after time of initial date and not less than three weeks after time of initial date.

c. **Following a bad date**

   1. **Responsibilities.** If upon completion of the first date a man sees no grounds to merit further pursuit of potential romantic interest, he shall be held under no obligation to ever call her.

   2. **Rights.** If a man, having completed a date which indicates no further romantic potentialities, refrains from calling

Discussion Points

After reading carefully through Section III, think about the following questions, or talk them over with a friend:

—Do you think it's fair that women and men are held to different rules while dating?

—What do you think anyone could do about it?

—Have you ever dated someone who held back a very important secret from you that you wish you had known about? How did that make you feel?

—What's the most intimate you've ever gotten with someone on a first date?

—Did you feel gross afterward?

—Do you think you'd do it again? Soon?

or otherwise contacting the woman with whom said date was undertaken, he shall not be held liable to scorn, contempt, bitching, ragging, or whining by said woman, by her friends or colleagues, or by mutual acquaintances of the parties involved.

ii. **Expression of Intent by the Woman**

a. If a woman has judged a first date to merit further exploration, she may express her feelings by

1. Thanking the man for the date, upon receiving his follow-up call

2. Stating a desire to do a similar activity again in the near future

b. If, upon completion of a first date, a woman determines that she does not wish to pursue any further romantic possibilities with the man in question, she may, during the course of his initial follow-up call

    1. Suggest that they remain friends.

    2. Indicate that she will be so busy in the immediate future that further socializing will be impossible.

    3. Tell him frankly that she never wishes to see him again.

    4. Hang up.

c. Regardless of whether a female feels a date was good, suboptimal, or bad, she shall under no circumstances whatsoever call, email, fax, phone, or contact through third-party intermediaries the man with whom the date was undertaken, unless he has left her a message specifically indicating that she do so.

Section IV:
Early Courtship

OVERVIEW: *The first few dates of a relationship have been likened to the beginning of a horse race: It is a time of acceleration and growing excitement, when momentum is building for what could be a triumphal conclusion—or a headlong tumble into disaster. At no point are finely honed dating skills as essential. Some fear and dread this crucial period; others revel in the newness and sense of surprise. On the bright side: After a first date, daters can afford one another a good deal more latitude in what's said and done.*

A. **Pursuit-of-Options Period (POP)**
   i. **Definition.** The POP is the time of low-intensity, responsibility-free exploration which occurs early in a romantic relationship. It is characterized by a freedom to pursue external romantic potentialities, while at the same time exploring the possible benefits and disadvantages of the relationship in question. The duration of the POP is as follows:

   a. **Beginning.** The POP begins at the successful completion of a first date.

   b. **Termination.** The POP runs until either of the following occurs:

   1. The establishment of a Mutually Agreed State of Dating, or MAD *(note: see* UDR&B *Sec. V.A.iv)*

   2. The withdrawal of the parties from the state of romantic

Dating Tip

It's okay to use affectionate expressions during the POP. You can call someone "sweetie" well before you can call them "my sweetie."

exploration *(note: see* UDR&B *Sec. IV.C.ii, "Exit Strategies," below)*

ii. **Terminology**

a. **"Dating."** Although the term "dating" is colloquially used to refer to single heterosexual romantic exploration in general, it may not be used to refer specifically to any POP relationship. The term "going out" also may not be used. Acceptable alternatives include

1. "Seeing"
2. "Hanging around with"
3. "Spending a lot of time with"

b. **"Boyfriend"/"girlfriend."** Terms which imply even a moderate degree of commitment, such as "boyfriend," "girlfriend," and the like, are not considered acceptable terms during the POP. Also unacceptable:

1. "My sweetie"
2. "My sweetheart"
3. "My cutie"
4. "My main squeeze"
5. "My man"/"woman"
6. "Mujer"
7. "Lover"

ADA Case Study

Jason, twenty-four, was working in the accounts receivable department of a large auto insurance firm. Janice, twenty-three, worked a couple of cubicles down. Janice is buxom and flirtatious, with a tattoo of Trix the Rabbit on her left shoulder that she got during spring break a few years back. Jason is thin and wiry, with long pale brown hair he wears pulled back in a ponytail with a rubber band. His tattoo is of an oriental ideogram that signifies "danger."

Though they had nearly nothing in common, Jason and Janice both immediately sensed a mutual sexual attraction, and once or twice a month they found themselves meeting for a drink after work, and then retreating to her place for a brief but ferocious interlude of drunken coupling.

After this had been going on for about two months, Janice dropped by Jason's cubicle one Wednesday afternoon and started dropping hints that she wanted him to take her out to dinner on Saturday night. Jason, taken aback, stammered a demurral but was too flustered to put together a coherent reply. Later in the day, though, when she stopped by to bug him again, he let her have it with both barrels, telling her that she was way out of line.

Janice burst into tears and fled back to her cubicle. Seeking solace, she reached into her desk drawer for her copy of the Green Book, which helped refresh her memory as to the provisions of *UDR&B* Sec. IV.A.iii.b, "Claims on time periods." Realizing that she had overstepped her bounds, she later apologized to Jason, and their parasexual friendship continued in a mutually satisfactory manner.

c. **"Friend."** Terms which imply no level of commitment at all are acceptable during the POP. These include, but are not limited to

1. "Friend"
2. "Good friend"
3. "Special friend"
4. "This person I know"

iii. **Invitations for Dates**

a. **Frequency.** During the POP, neither party shall be held responsible for

1. Frequency of invitations for dates
2. Frequency of dates

b. **Claims on time periods.** Neither POP partner shall expect, or lay claim to, certain periods of the week, e.g., Friday or Saturday night, or expect

1. To be invited on dates during said times
2. To be notified of the other party's plans during said times

c. **Extension of invitations**

1. Either party in a POP relationship may extend an invitation to go on a date. *(Note: Cf.* UDR&B *Sec. III.A.i.a.)*
2. The following shall not be deemed suitable venues for POP dates: weddings; funerals; office parties; religious retreats; cruises or foreign trips in excess of three days' duration.
3. Invitations shall be extended no later than twenty-four hours before the proposed meeting time, and no earlier than seven days before the proposed meeting time.
4. Either party in a POP relationship is at full liberty to refuse any invitation to go on a date, for any reason.
5. By declining an invitation to go on a date, a person shall not expect to signal, nor shall he or she be understood to

have signaled, a desire never to see the other party again. *(Note: Cf.* UDR&B *Sec. III.A.iv.d.)*

iv. **Use of the Telephone**

a. **Multiple unilateral calls.** The placing of multiple unilateral calls is not permissible. Having placed a telephone call to his or her POP partner, and having either talked with said partner or left a message, a person shall not then call again until

> **Dating Haiku**
> **"Waiting for a Call"**
>
> Phone sits on sofa
> Cord tangled as my heartstrings
> O Ring, god damned you!
>
> —G. Lauroncia Bigelow,
> *A Different Shade of Night,*
> Firelight Publishing,
> Seattle, 1996

1. Said POP partner has returned the call.

2. A legitimately urgent issue has arisen, such as the sudden need to leave town for a long period of time, which if not communicated could threaten the nascent relationship. *(Note: Care must be taken not to confuse imaginary urgent issues, such as a sudden irrational fear that one's POP partner has somehow lost one's phone number, with actual urgent issues.)*

b. **Frequency**

1. There shall be no limit on the frequency with which partners in a POP relationship may call each other, subject to provision *UDR&B* Sec. IV.A.iv.a, above.

2. If a member of a POP relationship does not call within one (1) week of the last conversation, or make any equivalent attempt to reestablish contact within said time period, the POP shall be deemed to have ended. *(Note: See* UDR&B *Sec. IV.C.ii.b.7, below.)*

v. **Other Potentialities**

a. **Nonexclusivity.** During the POP, neither party shall be excluded from pursuing any number of other romantic potentialities, nor shall either expect the other to refrain from such pursuits.

b. **Special partner exclusion.** While neither party shall be constrained from pursuing any and all other romantic potentialities, the following shall not, out of consideration for human sensitivities, be acceptable subjects for romantic exploration:

1. Partner's friends
2. Partner's colleagues
3. Partner's relatives
4. Partner's roommates

vi. **Gifts**

a. **Forbidden.** Neither party shall for any reason make excessively large gifts, defined as having

---

ADA Case Study

In September 1987, Eunice LaForge, a twenty-four-year-old editorial assistant at a major women's magazine, began spending time romantically with Gus Stanley, a twenty-nine-year-old editor at an automotive monthly owned by the same corporation. A month later Stanley began seeing Shawnette Hawkins, another editor at his magazine. LaForge filed a Rogue Dater petition with the ADA, complaining that Stanley had violated the special partner exclusion of the POP rules, specifically *UDR&B* Sec. IV.A.v.b.2.

In its subsequent ruling declining Ms. LaForge's petition, the ADA Compliance Division Review Panel offered a narrow interpretation of the "colleague" provision, ruling that persons employed in different offices of the same firm could not be considered "colleagues" for this purpose.

    1. A cash value in excess of four hours' wages

    2. Culturally powerful meaning, such as framed photographs of self, a ring, etc.

b. **Acceptable.** Parties may make small gifts of essentially benign character, so long as they are not made with excessive frequency or with overeffusive displays of emotion. Acceptable gifts include

    1. Flowers

    2. Alcohol, especially wine

    3. Candy

    4. Small stuffed animals

    5. Unframed photographs of neutral subject matters

vii. **Holidays and Special Occasions**

a. **Holidays.** No special expectations regarding holidays shall be entertained by POP partners, with the following exceptions:

    1. **Christmas.** If the POP overlaps Christmas, a small gift may be made, but no gift shall be expected. *(Note: See* UDR&B *Sec. IV.A.vi.a, above.)*

    2. **Valentine's Day.** POP partners shall avoid all contact in the ninety-six hours preceding Valentine's Day, a "blackout period" of pre-dating heterosexual socialization.

b. **Birthdays.** If the POP overlaps with either partner's birthday, the other party may make no more than two of the following three gestures, and is obliged to make none:

    1. Offer to take the celebrant to dinner.

    2. Give the celebrant an inscribed greeting card.

    3. Give the celebrant a small gift. *(Note: Please refer to* UDR&B *Sec. IV.A.vi.b, "Gifts, Acceptable," above.)*

c. **Parties**

    1. Neither party in a POP relationship shall expect to auto-

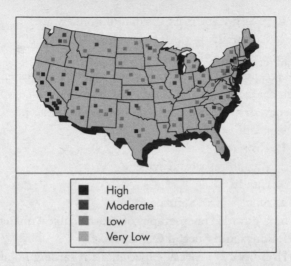

Fig. IV.1. Geographical Distribution of Reluctant POP Gift Givers. The question of whether individuals in the earliest stages of courtship should give holiday gifts is considered by relationship scientists to be one of the field's most vexing issues. In an attempt to shed light on regional viewpoints, 14,000 single heterosexuals around the nation were polled as to what they would do if they were dating someone for two weeks and Christmas rolled around. Areas in light gray show counties where a low percentage (<20 percent) said they would not give a present. Areas in black show counties where a high percentage (>67 percent) responded similarly. *Source:* "Early Courtship: An Untapped Resource?" *Journal of Marketing Science,* February 1998.

matically be invited to all parties of which their partner is aware.

2. If two members of a POP relationship run into one another at a party or other social function, they shall not be obliged to leave together, nor to treat the occasion as an incipient crisis.

    d. **Pseudo-anniversaries.** Pseudo-anniversaries, such as one-week and and one-month "anniversaries," shall not be celebrated by POP partners. *(Note: Cf. UDR&B Sec. V.D.ii.c.)*

viii. **Negotiation.** At no time during a POP shall either party bring up or attempt to discuss

    a. The relationship

    b. How his or her POP partner feels about him or her in the long term

    c. Marriage, children, or growing old

    d. Any topic that smacks of intensive commitment and hence should properly be left for the next phase of the relationship, the Mutually Agreed State of Dating, should it occur *(note: see* UDR&B *Sec. V, "Advanced Courtship")*

B. First Sex

i. Time of Occurrence

    a. **Early.** There shall be no miminum time before which sex may not occur in a relationship. *(Note: However, see* UDR&B *Sec. III.C.iv.)*

    b. **Mean.** Parties shall understand that the mean time before sexual congress among single heterosexual Americans is 3.1 dates, with the following provisos:

        1. The fact that this number of dates has not yet occurred shall not in itself be taken as justification to avoid sex.

        2. The fact that this number of dates has been exceeded shall not in itself be taken as justification to pressure for sex.

    c. **Late.** If no sex has been forthcoming after seven dates, then both parties shall put aside any expectations that it may someday occur. *(Note: See Fig. IV.2. Sexualized nonintercourse relationships are deemed noncompliant by the American Dating Association. Readers are advised that similar topics are covered in a pamphlet issued by the National*

Friendship Society, "So, Your Resolutely Platonic Friend Enjoys Turning You On?")

ii. **Quality**

a. **Remediable shortcomings.** Being that the first time a couple have sex is often fraught with expectation and nervousness, the following shall not be deemed to reflect poorly on the partner exhibiting them:

1. Fumbling
2. Excessive haste
3. Clumsiness
4. Impotence
5. Vaginal dryness
6. Premature ejaculation

b. **Irremediable shortfalls.** Because the following shortcomings cannot be fixed, they may be deemed sufficient cause to rethink the value of a romantic potentiality:

1. Excessively small or large genitals
2. Surprising or inappropriate hirsuteness
3. Supernumerary or unidentifiable appendages
4. Erogenous zone tatooed with someone else's name
5. Profound psychosexual or behavioral dysfunction, e.g., insisting on wearing diapers during intercourse.

c. **Kinkiness.** Neither party shall attempt erotic explorations of an advanced nature during a first instance of sexual intercourse.

iii. **Birth Control.** For the first act of sexual intercourse, and for any subsequent act of sexual penetration during the POP, a man must wear a condom, notwithstanding

a. Any simultaneous use of other birth control methods by the woman

b. Previous sexual history of the partners, whether claimed or actual

c. Sterility of either partner, claimed or actual

d. Recent negative STD tests, claimed or actual

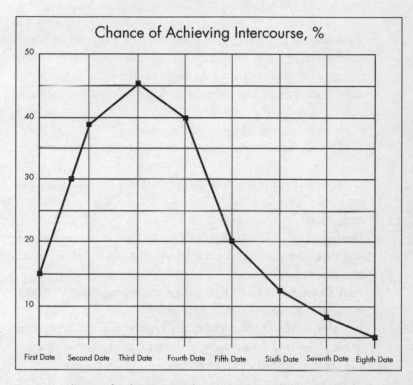

Fig. IV.2. Chance of Achieving Initial Sexual Relations. The probability that first-time intercourse will occur is plotted against the number of the POP date in question. The mean number of dates before first sex in the U.S. currently stands at 3.1, which coincides nontrivially with the probability peak. *Source:* "Multiphasic Analysis of Single Heterosexual Dating Behavior," *United States Census Bureau,* 2000.

Rule of Thumb

If you aren't turned on the first time you have sex with someone, the odds are it isn't going to get better later on.

iv. **Spending the Night.** Upon completion of a first act of sexual intercourse, or upon completion of any act of sexual intercourse during a POP, no person may presume the right to spend the night at another person's dwelling. A person may stay the night only if

a. He or she is invited to spend the night.

b. He or she is the current owner or tenant of the home in question.

c. He or she is the tenant or owner's guest, and the tenant or owner has fallen asleep.

C. **Termination**

i. **Timing.** The POP is a fundamentally limited, short-term period of exploration, and shall be understood to last no more than three months.

ii. **Exit Strategies.** The POP deadline having expired, the parties involved may choose one of two options:

a. **Enter a MAD.** The Pursuit-of-Options Period having expired, partners choose to intensify their relationship by entering a Mutually Agreed State of Dating. *(Note: See* UDR&B *Sec. V, "Advanced Courtship.")*

b. **Terminate the relationship.** *(Note: In common parlance, ending any romantic relationship is termed "breaking up." Technically, however, one cannot break up in a POP relationship because one is not technically dating.)* Acceptable forms of termination include

1. In person
2. Sending a bouquet of flowers with a note
3. Telephoning
4. Sending a letter
5. Sending a fax
6. Sending an email
7. Not ever calling again or returning phone calls

Discussion Points

After reading carefully through Section IV, think about the following questions, or talk them over with a friend:

—Have you ever spent time with someone, and then found out later that they thought you were dating, and it hadn't even crossed your mind? How did that make you feel?

—Sometimes the early stages of a relationship can be like shopping for groceries. Folk wisdom tells us that one should never go grocery shopping on an empty stomach. How would you rewrite this adage to apply to dating?

—What do the great works of world literature have to tell us about the POP phase of courtship?

—What if time went backward, and people started out married, and then they got engaged, and then they dated, and then they went through the POP, and then they didn't even know each other? How weird would that be?

—The motto of the State of New Hampshire is "Live free or die." Do you think this motto could also apply to relationships?

Section V:
Advanced Courtship

OVERVIEW: *According to ADA statistics, 76 percent of all single heterosexual Americans currently consider themselves to be dating. But what exactly does "dating" mean? In technical terms, you aren't really dating unless you have entered what is termed a "Mutually Agreed State of Dating," or MAD. In this chapter, we elucidate the rights and responsibilities that go along with a serious, MAD relationship.*

A. **Mutually Agreed State of Dating (MAD)**
   i. **Definition.** A couple shall be deemed to have entered into a Mutually Agreed State of Dating (MAD) when they have both explicitly agreed not to pursue romantic potentialities with any other parties and to identify themselves as "dating." The duration of the MAD is constrained as follows:

   a. **Beginning.** The MAD begins at the moment both parties explicitly assent to its existence.

   b. **Termination.** The MAD runs until one of the following occurs:

   1. The breakup of the parties involved *(note: see* UDR&B *Sec. IX, "Termination")*
   2. Engagement
   3. Marriage
   4. The death or permanent disappearance of either or both parties

ii. **Terminology.** The terminology proper to the MAD differs in some respects to that of a non-MAD state.

a. **"Dating."** Parties involved in a MAD relationship may describe their condition as any or all of the following:

    1. "Dating"

    2. "Going out with"

    3. Any other term which connotes a significant but non-binding level of commitment

b. **"Hanging around."** Parties involved in a MAD relationship may not refer to their condition as

    1. "Hanging around"

    2. "Spending time with"

    3. "Seeing"

    4. Any other term with minimal or nugatory connotations of commitment

c. **"Boyfriend"/"girlfriend."** Members of a MAD relationship may and shall refer to one another by terms confirming their mutual exclusivity. Such terms include

    1. "Boyfriend"/"girlfriend"

    2. "My guy"/"my girl"

    3. "Sweetheart"

    4. "Sweetie"

    5. "My man"/"my woman"

d. **"Friend."** Having entered into a MAD, neither party shall again refer to the other as any of the following, so long as the state of MAD shall continue to obtain:

    1. "Friend"

    2. "Good friend"

    3. "Special friend"

    4. "This person I know"

iii. **Onset**

  a. **Leading indicators.** Indications that a MAD ought to be established include

   1. Feelings of intense discomfort at the thought of one's POP partner engaging in romantic activities with someone else

   2. A deep-rooted feeling, whether rational or instinctive, that one's POP partner might be someone with whom one could spend one's life

   3. A realization that the three-month deadline for the expiration of the POP is coming soon *(note: see* UDR&B *Sec. IV.C.i.),* and that one does not want the relationship to terminate

   4. Heavy, incessant, and irresistible pressure from one's POP partner for the establishment of a MAD

Dating Tip

Has the prospect of going for the full commitment got you tongue-tied? Try this tried-and-tested formula.

"(Partner's name here), I've really gotten attached to you. So much so that I don't want to see anybody else. Do you feel the same way?"

According to the Men's Action Network, which has honed and perfected this formula over decades of intensive field testing, the best time to use this line is immediately after a round of orgasmic sex, particularly at the culmination of a long, romantic evening. Alcohol also helps, both in getting out the question and in generating the desired response.

---

b. **Prequalification.** No party shall be eligible for a MAD if he or she

   1. Is not currently engaged in a POP relationship

   2. Is already noncompliant with the terms of the POP relationship

   3. Does not understand the obligations of a MAD relationship

   4. Understands the obligations of a MAD relationship but has no intention of living up to them

iv. **Initiation of MAD**

a. **Time window.** There is no minimum time requirement prior to the establishment of a MAD. *Example: For instance, a MAD agreement might conceivably occur on a first date.*

b. **Explicit assent.** The MAD shall only be deemed established if both parties knowingly and willingly consent to its establishment. This discussion may take any mutually agreeable form, including

   1. Joint agreement, freely arrived at

   2. Ultimatum and capitulation

c. **Terminological equivalence.** If the parties in a relationship agree to any of the terms of a MAD, they shall be deemed to have agreed to all of them. *Example: For instance, if a man and a woman agree that they are "dating," they are by that fact also bound to the principle of exclusivity.*

d. **Exclusion of tacit arrangements.** A MAD may never be entered into tacitly. *Example: For instance, if a man knows, and is known to know, that a woman with whom he has gone on dates is widely and frequently claiming to be his girlfriend, his failure to inform her otherwise does not in itself indicate that a MAD is in effect.*

When Did You Establish Your MAD?

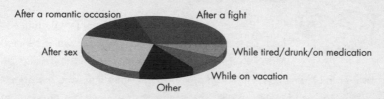

Fig. V.1. When Did You Establish Your MAD? A 1998 poll of 1,200 single American heterosexuals who self-identified as MAD partners revealed that a plurality of 32 percent had established their MAD after a fight. This finding is consistent with the epinephrine-serotonin theory of behavioral dynamics, which holds that intense emotional states like anger, fear, and love are often interchangeable.

An alternative explanation is that capitulation to a partner's MAD-seeking demands might often be used as a conflict-avoidance strategy. *Source: ADA Bi-Annual Polyaxial Attitude Survey,* Spring/Summer 1998.

   e. **Sobriety**
      1. It is not necessary that either party be sober, fully awake, or taking any necessary medications during the establishment of the MAD for the agreement to be considered valid.
      2. No party shall claim mental incapacitation on any grounds as an excuse to plea for reversion from MAD to POP. *(Note: See* UDR&B *Sec. V.A.v.a, below.)*
  v. **Irreversibility**
   a. A MAD having been established, neither party may decide unilaterally to revert to a POP state without telling the other party, e.g., for the purpose of investigating another dating potentiality.

ADA Case Study

Philip Preston, thirty-two, was a self-employed architectural consultant living in New York City when he met Maebeth Ralston, a twenty-nine-year-old journalist, at a party in the Hamptons. They had sex the night they met, and thereafter were together nearly every night. Their relationship was both passionate and fiery; Maebeth was prone to short but intense bouts of anger, and frequently resorted to throwing things across the room.

Despite the storminess of their relationship, Philip and Maebeth enjoyed a convivial social life, meeting frequently with both his friends and hers after work and on weekends. Though they never actually talked about where their relationship was headed, Philip began to suspect that Maebeth could be "the one," a feeling he had not experienced since a devastating breakup with a Singapore Airlines stewardess when he was in his mid-twenties.

Philip and Maebeth had been dating for nearly four weeks when Philip learned that Maebeth was also seeing a lawyer she had met earlier in the summer. Philip was outraged—wasn't she betraying his trust?

In his pain and confusion, Philip called the ADA and was put in touch with a Dating Assistance Counselor. Over the course of their conversation, Philip realized that he had failed to establish a Mutually Agreed State of Dating, and so Maebeth was fully within her rights in seeing other men. Upon the counselor's suggestion, Philip invited Maebeth to enter a MAD with him. She agreed. Today, they are still together and happily cohabiting.

b. If a party, having entered into a MAD, decides unilaterally to revert to a POP state, the relationship shall be deemed to have ended. *(Note: See* UDR&B *Sec. IX, "Termination.")*

c. A MAD having been established, the Principle of Irreversibility shall henceforth apply in all dealings between members of the couple in question, namely:

1. The relationship may not revert from a more advanced stage of commitment to a less advanced stage.

2. Should the relationship terminate, it shall not commence again.

vi. **Variants**

a. **Long-distance dating.** If parties in a MAD maintain a primary residence in different municipalities, counties, states, or countries, to such an extent that travel time between them prevents the said parties from seeing each other more than twice per month, then they shall be deemed Long-Distance Daters. While this type of relationship is officially sanctioned by the ADA, daters shall be aware of the following advantages and disadvantages:

1. **Advantages.** Among the advantages of long-distance dating are an enhanced sense of freshness and novelty at each encounter; an increased resistance to petty irritations caused by the other party's idiosyncracies and bad habits; and a greater use of the imagination to enhance the mystery and suspense of the unfolding relationship.

2. **Disadvantages.** Among the disadvantages of long-distance dating are an attenuated sense of familiarity with the other party; increased feelings of loneliness, boredom, and sexual dissatisfaction; disproportionately high telephone and transportation costs; heightened suspicions that one is

unappreciated and unloved; and an increased predilection for cheating.

b. **Open relationship.** If, having surpassed the maximum POP time limit of three months, the dating partners decide that they wish to increase the level of commitment in their relationship, but that this commitment shall not include sexual exclusivity, then they shall be deemed to have entered into an open relationship. Such relationships are not compatible with the terms of a MAD and are not sanctioned by the ADA. *(Note: Daters seeking to*

A Closer Look: You've Heard About PCS

It seems that Pseudo Commitment Syndrome, or PCS, is all the rage these days. You can't turn on a television or look at a newspaper headline without confronting its catchy acronym. But what exactly is it?

In simple terms, PCS refers to a powerful male dating strategy of appearing to be committed to a woman, without actually saying so, or being so. Its hallmark is phrases like "you're so special" or "you're everything to me," without concomitant promises like "I will not date anyone but you." A woman is left under the impression that she is in an exclusive relationship, but, using the loophole presented by *UDR&B* Sec. V.A.iv.d, the male has deceptively kept the relationship in the POP stage.

Relationships scientists have only in recent years begun to understand just how widespread this phenomenon is. Once PCS springs its terrible trap, few relationships can withstand its devastation. Are you at risk? If you're not sure, then you very well may be. Only one cure is effective: To make sure your man is exclusively committed to you, make sure he says so explicitly.

learn more about open relationships should contact the Swingers' Support Network, a branch of the Alternative Lifestyle Coalition.)

B. **Exclusivity**

  i. **Definition.** Exclusivity shall be understood to prohibit the undertaking of any of the following activities with a third party:

  a. **Sexual intercourse** *(note: see* UDR&B *Sec. I, "sex")*

  b. **Sexual behavior** *(note: see* UDR&B *Sec. I, "sexual behavior")*

  c. **Phone sex** *(note: see* UDR&B *Sec VI.G.iii.)*

  d. **Pursuit of other romantic potentialities.** Neither party shall pursue other romantic potentialities, as by actively flirting, asking other parties on dates, going on dates, placing classified ads, and so forth.

  ii. **Prohibited Behaviors.** The following behaviors shall be deemed unacceptable during a MAD under the provisions of exclusivity:

  a. **Exes.** Neither party shall keep displayed on the wall, affixed to the refrigerator, on his or her desk at work, or atop furniture at home

   1. Photographs of any ex
   2. Artworks produced by any ex
   3. Evocative mementoes of any ex

  b. **Time alone with third parties.** Neither member of a MAD relationship shall spend an inordinate amount of time alone with any other eligible member of the opposite sex, or spend time alone together with any other eligible member of the opposite sex in an erotically charged atmosphere, as for instance

   1. Spending the night together in the same room
   2. Going off alone together on vacation
   3. Going skinny-dipping alone together
   4. Going to strip clubs together

REMEMBER

Noncompliant daters void their dating rights!

c. **Unnecessary physicality.** Neither party shall engage in unnecessary physicality with any other eligible member of the opposite sex, including

1. Solicitation, offer, or administration of backrubs or other massages
2. Lingering hugs
3. Over-the-clothing fondles
4. Kisses on the lips, with or without the insertion of tongue

d. **Excessive gawking.** No party shall gawk excessively at any other eligible member of the opposite sex. Excessive shall be defined as stares involving

1. Continuous concentration of more than ten seconds duration
2. A slackness of the jaw
3. A sudden jerking of the head

iii. **Acceptable Behaviors.** The following shall be deemed acceptable within the framework of a MAD:

a. **An attitude of openness.** As parties in a MAD remain single, and are not married to each other, neither party shall feel constrained from keeping an eye out for another potential dating partner with whom he or she might enjoy a more fruitful and fulfilling relationship. *(Note: The potential discovery of such a person does not relieve a party of their obligations under the exclusivity provisions of the* Universal Dating Regulations & Bylaws. *See* UDR&B *Sec. IX.B.i.a.5.)*

b. **Platonic friendships.** No party shall be enjoined from maintaining strictly platonic friendships, so long as said friendships

    1. Are truly platonic

    2. Are not intended as preambles to potential future relationships *(note: see* UDR&B *Sec. II.A.ii.e)*

    3. Do not involve unnecessary physicality *(note: see* UDR&B *Sec. V.B.ii.c, above)*

    4. Do not involve spending more time together than with actual dating partner

    5. Do not involve greater degrees of emotional or physical intimacy than with actual dating partner

c. **Contact with exes.** Parties shall not be enjoined from maintaining infrequent contact with any exes with whom they remain friendly provided

    1. Such contact remains within the bounds of propriety. *(Note: See* UDR&B *Sec. V.B.ii, above.)*

    2. Neither party entertains thoughts or intentions of rekindling the prior relationship.

    3. Neither party disparages the current relationship, nor compares it unfavorably to any past relationship.

    4. No disparaging, intimate, or ridiculous anecdotes or stories are told about the current partner.

d. **Memorabilia.** Provided that such items are not openly placed on display, or kept in a place where they might easily be accidentally found, no person shall be enjoined from keeping

    1. Old love letters and other memorabilia related to previous relationships or dating partners

    2. Diaries

    3. Electronic media recordings of or relating to former dating partners, including videotapes of sexual acts

iv. **Jealousy**

a. No party shall be excessively possessive, jealous, or obsessive about his or her dating partner.

b. No person shall ask questions about past exes, romances, feelings, or experiences, unless he or she is prepared to deal with the answer free of recriminations.

c. No person shall be constrained to give truthful answers concerning

1. Matters which are not obligated to fully disclose the truth about *(note: see* UDR&B *Sec. III.B.iv)*

2. Matters which they reasonably expect the other person will not be able to handle the truth about

d. Neither party shall look through the other party's personal effects looking for information on past relationships or liaisons.

e. No person shall invite comparison between him or herself and past dating partners.

f. Neither party shall intentionally do things to make the other party jealous

1. For the sake of gauging the intensity of their affections

2. To punish them for a perceived slight

3. For the sake of boosting their own esteem

4. For the hell of it

C. **Other Rights and Obligations**

i. **Invitations for Dates**

a. **Initiation**

1. Either party in a MAD relationship may extend an invitation to spend time together.

2. Invitations may be extended at any time, with any amount of advance notice, for any type of activity, so long as said activity is *UDR&B* compliant.

Rule of Thumb

The more habitually jealous someone is, the more likely he or she is to cheat on you.

3. Either party may decline an invitation to spend time together without explanation or recrimination, and the act of declining said invitation shall not in and of itself be interpreted as a lack of enthusiasm for the relationship as a whole.

b. **Frequency**

1. There is no limit to how much time members of a MAD relationship may spend together. *(Note: See* UDR&B *Sec. V.C.ii.a.3.)*

2. Members of a MAD relationship must see each other no less than once per week, unless they are living in different cities. *(Note: See* UDR&B *Sec. V.A.vi.a, "Long-distance dating.")*

c. **Claims on time periods.** Members of a MAD relationship, if they are not scheduled to spend Friday and Saturday night together, are entitled to a true and full accounting of their partners' activities. Note that

1. Partners are not required to submit documentary evidence of said activity.

2. Claiming to have drunk so much that one forgot what one did last night is not deemed to qualify as adequate accounting.

d. **Use of the telephone.** Members of a MAD relationship may call one another as often as either wishes, without needing to wait for the other party to call back first. However:

1. Calls shall not be placed so frequently to a partner's workplace that he or she becomes the butt of jokes.

2. Members of a dating relationship shall remember that not every detail of one's daily life needs to be immediately related and expounded upon at length to one's partner.

ii. **Clarity of Intentions.** Each party shall articulate as clearly as possible his or her views regarding the relationship.

a. **Intensity.** Each party shall articulate his or her desired level of intensity for the relationship according to the following:

1. **Light.** Parties see each other an average of once per week.

2. **Moderate.** Parties see each other two or three times per week.

3. **Heavy.** Parties see each other four or five times per week. *(Note: Parties wishing to see each other more than five times per week should consult* UDR&B *Sec. VII, "Moving In.")*

b. **Commitment**

1. If a person has no intention of maintaining the relationship in the long term, he or she must reveal this fact as soon as it occurs to him or her.

2. If, after one (1) year, either party has still not decided whether they may wish to pursue the relationship in the long term, it may be presumed by the other party that he or she never will.

c. **Ultimatums**

1. Either party, frustrated by his or her partner's failure to communicate on the subject of commitment, may issue threats in order to compel such communication.

2. If the other party does not meet the conditions of said ultimatum, the threat must be applied in full measure.

ADA Case Study

In 1993 Laura Gibbs, a thirty-two-year-old receptionist working at an international shoe company, demanded that her boyfriend of four years, Larry Maverick, propose marriage. When he proved reluctant, she threatened to leave him if he didn't propose by the end of the month. The end of the month came and went, and eventually the matter was dropped.

A little over a year later, Laura and Larry voluntarily entered ADA dating arbitration over an unrelated matter. Laura was on the verge of winning a verdict in that case when Larry brought to the Arbitration Board's attention the fact that Laura had issued an unfulfilled ultimatum. Since her violation predated Larry's later noncompliance, the board ruled in Larry's favor.

"If an ultimatum is issued that might end a relationship, and its terms are not met," the Board wrote, "then as far as proper procedure is concerned, the relationship is over, whether the ultimatum's issuer wishes it or not."

iii. **Disposition.** Both parties shall strive to maintain an upbeat emotional atmosphere within the context of the MAD relationship.

a. **Pleasantness.** Parties shall strive to minimize the following behaviors, particularly in the presence of friends or family:

1. Harrassing
2. Complaining
3. Whining
4. Berating
5. Brow-beating
6. Haranguing
7. Nagging

b. **Discretion.** Each party shall attempt to the full extent of his or her abilities to keep information regarding the relationship, including but not limited to descriptions of sexual activities and embarrassing personal habits, to himself or herself, and not share it on the sly with other friends.

c. **Empathy.** Each member of a MAD relationship shall attempt to fully deploy their empathic capabilities in order to

1. Understand and console when a partner has setbacks or difficulties, whether trivial or profound.

2. Express happiness and demonstrate true enthusiasm for a partner's victories or windfalls, of whatever nature.

3. Minimize or eliminate feelings of jealousy, envy, or insecurity regarding the other party's good fortune.

4. Understand, and when possible fulfill, the needs, hopes, and desires of his or her partner.

5. Cut him or her a little slack, especially when he or she is taking a nap.

d. **Honesty.** Both parties shall strive to tell the truth as often as is feasible. *(Note: See* UDR&B *Sec. V.B.iv.c, above.)*

e. **Honor.** Neither member of a MAD relationship shall abuse his or her partner's trust by treating him or her in scandalous or disreputable ways, including but not limited to

1. Secretly taking dirty pictures

2. Spreading false or malicious rumors about him or her

3. Using him or her as the basis for an unsympathetic character in a scandalous roman à clef novel, film script, or teleplay

f. **Attentiveness**

1. Each member of a MAD relationship shall endeavor to contact his or her partner, either electronically or in person, on a frequent basis.

Pop Quiz

Match the obligation with its violation.

1. Exclusivity
2. Discretion
3. Pleasantness
4. Empathy
5. Honesty
6. Attentiveness

a. Complaining about her taste in music
b. Telling his friends she craves unorthodox sexual acts
c. Sulking because her raise means she earns more
d. Telling her he had two drinks when he really had six
e. Going on a week's vacation and forgetting to call
f. Implying to an attractive female coworker that he's single

Answers: 1. f 2. b 3. a 4. c 5. d 6. e

2. Neither party shall avoid contact with his or her dating partner for more than three (3) days for any reason whatsoever.

3. Each member shall attempt, as much as possible, to listen to what the other person is talking about.

iv. **Spending the Night**

a. A member of a MAD relationship shall not be asked to leave his or her partner's home after sex, being entitled to spend the night if he or she so wishes.

b. A member of a MAD relationship may choose not to spend the night at a partner's house after sex if he or she so wishes.

c. A member of a MAD relationship shall be entitled to keep a reasonable number of small personal effects at his or her partner's house, including

1. Toothbrush
2. Hairbrush

**Dating Haiku
"Togetherness"**

Beside the Pepto
One red toothbrush, one yellow
And a box of floss

—G. Laurencia Bigelow,
Dreams, Clouds and Whispers,
Firelight Publishing,
Seattle, 1987

3. Contact lens solution
4. Any number of necessary medications
5. No more than six (6) toiletries

d. Regardless of who has to leave for work or school first, the MAD partner who is visiting may not presume to stay on in the home or apartment after his or her host has left for the day. *(Note: However, the guest may stay if an invitation to do so is freely extended by the host.)*

D. Romance

i. Terms of Endearment

a. **Pet names.** Upon establishment of a MAD, parties may gradually begin to address one another in the form of pet names, including but not limited to the following:

1. Boo
2. Woo
3. Goo
4. Bub-bub
5. Puggles
6. Cuddlums
7. Any other combination of nonsense syllables which handily connotes a feeling of childlike vulnerability and openness

(Note: No person shall apply a pet name to his or her partner which he or she has used previously to refer to an ex-boyfriend or ex-girlfriend.)

b. **Baby talk.** The use of baby talk in a MAD relationship is permissible, with the following limitations:

1. It shall be used sparingly.
2. It shall not be used despite the obvious irritation of one's partner.

3. It shall not be used in the presence of any other persons.

c. **The "L" word**

1. It is not permissible for a MAD to persist more than six months without each party either explicitly expressing his or her love for the other or stating his or her desire to end the relationship.

2. If a person is informed that his or her party loves him or her, he or she has two weeks to either respond in kind or state his or her desire to end the relationship.

ii. **Holidays and Special Occasions**

a. **Valentine's Day**

1. Valentine's Day shall be reserved exclusively and solely to be spent with one's MAD relationship partner, particularly dinner and its aftermath.

2. Dinner shall be arranged and paid for by the male member of the relationship.

3. At least two of the following shall also be provided by the male: card; chocolates; flowers; lingerie; perfume.

4. If the female member of the MAD relationship has any reason to fault the quality of the dinner or the presents proferred by the male, she shall keep her criticisms to herself for the duration of the holiday.

5. Parties shall have sex on Valentine's Day unless prohibited by physical impossibility, as by the amputation of required organs or physical absence necessitated by the federal judicial system.

b. **Anniversaries**

1. The base date for purposes of establishing a couple's anniversary shall be defined as the date upon which they first

met; or, the date upon which they first went on a date; or, the date upon which they first had sex; or, the date upon which they first declared their desire for exclusive commitment; or any such mutually agreeable occasion.

2. The rules to be followed by members of a MAD relationship are identical to those for Valentine's Day. *(Note: See* UDR&B *Sec. V.D.ii.a, above.)*

c. **Pseudo-anniversaries**

1. Any couple too impatient to wait a full year before celebrating their togetherness, or too uncertain that their relationship will endure for such a long period of time, may celebrate the elapsing of a one-week, one-month, or six-month period of time from their relationship's base date, as they see fit. *(Note: See* UDR&B *Sec. V.D.ii.b.1, above.)*

2. Couples shall be free to establish whatever set of protocols they wish to follow regarding their pseudo-anniversary celebrations.

3. Neither party shall expect the celebration of pseudo-anniversaries to continue after the celebration of their first actual anniversary, though couples may agree to do so if they both so wish.

E. **Health, Hygiene, and Appearance**

i. **Hygiene.** If a member of a MAD relationship expects his or her partner to come over to his or her home, the following protocols shall be observed.

a. **Tidiness.** He or she shall maintain his or her apartment to within tolerable levels of order and cleanliness, including but not limited to the following criteria:

1. Dirty laundry, especially underwear, shall not be left on the floor.

Dating Tip

Be careful about giving expensive gifts too early in a relationship: Expectations always ratchet upward. Broke? Write her a note. She'll still be cherishing it long after any flowers would have wilted.

2. The toilet seat shall not be left up.

3. Dirty dishes shall not be left in the sink for more than forty-eight hours.

4. Uneaten food, except for uncut fruit, shall not be left exposed for more than four hours.

5. Stored food shall not be kept within forty-eight hours of the detection of mold, fungus, rot, etc.

6. No cobwebs shall be visible

7. No dead bugs in excess of 2 mm in length shall be visible.

8. The cockroach population shall be kept below one sighting per twenty-four-hour period.

9. Garbage, trash, and other refuse shall be disposed of in a time period not greater than the gestation period of a maggot egg in said partner's climatic zone.

ii. **Health and Appearance**

a. Each member of a MAD relationship shall take reasonable care to maintain his or her fitness and attractiveness.

b. Neither party shall excessively solicit compliments about his or her appearance.

c. Neither party shall solicit opinions unless they are prepared to accept the truth.

d. Neither party shall be unduly harsh in verbally appraising the other.

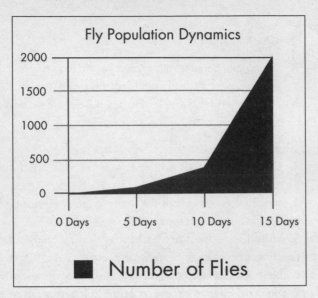

Fig. V.2. Population Dynamics of the Common Housefly, *Musca Domestica*. As is well known, houseflies provided adequate supplies of food can breed exponentially. A convenient and nutritious supply of such food can generally be found in the kitchen areas of bachelor living quarters. The ensuing swarms of living vermin help repel human females, ensuring the continued bachelorhood of the male, which ensures continued supplies of refuse for fly progeny to feed on. Thus the great circle of life continues. *Source:* Goldblum, J., "Parasite Interactions on the Socioanthropology of Human Reproduction," *Science*, Vol. VIII.

e. Neither party shall directly pressure the other to undergo a fitness regime.

iii. **Clothing**

a. A woman shall not excessively pester her male MAD relationship partner to wear

       1. A belt

       2. Matching shoes

       3. Any other clothing which subtly symbolizes the breaking of the male will

   b. A man, for the sake of pleasing his female MAD relationship partner, shall on select occasions make due effort to wear

       1. A belt

       2. Matching shoes

       3. Any other clothing which subtly signals his willingness to shoulder the responsibilities of a grown-up world

F. Friends and Family

i. Meeting

a. Friends

   1. **Timing.** If a person has not introduced his or her partner to his or her primary friends before the establishment of the MAD, he or she shall do so immediately subsequent to its establishment.

   2. **Exes.** A member of a MAD relationship is not permitted to introduce any ex-girlfriends or ex-boyfriends to his or her partner without express prior permission from said partner.

 Dating Tip

A sure sign that a partner is in love: His or her partner's disturbing habits or propensities, such as belly button lint or farting in the bathtub, are perceived as endearing.

Stat Attack

In 82 percent of instances where a person's friends and family vehemently despised his or her partner, they were ultimately proved to have been right. *Source: Asia-Pacific Economic Cooperation Taskforce Report, May 1998.*

b. **Family**

1. **Timing.** No person shall be required to introduce his or her partner to his or her family until he or she feels fully ready to do so, whether before, during, or after the period of MAD dating.

2. **Refusal.** No person shall refuse to meet a partner's family, unless doing so would require travel of more than ten hours' duration, or unless doing so would put them in physical or moral peril.

3. **Grooming.** When a man is preparing to meet his partner's family for the first time, he will take extra care to follow her advice on matters of clothing, grooming, and general appearance. When a woman is preparing to meet her partner's family for the first time, she will refrain from offering her partner such advice.

ii. **Subsequent Behavior**

a. **Criticism**

1. Criticism in front of partner's face. A member of a MAD relationship shall not permit his or her friends or family to openly criticize, demean, ridicule, or berate his or her partner.

2. Criticism behind partner's back. A member of a MAD relationship shall not encourage his or her friends or family to criticize, demean, ridicule, or berate his or her partner behind his or her back.

3. Of friends and family. No person shall persistently and maliciously disparage his or her partner's friends or family.

Discussion Points

After reading carefully through Section V, think about the following questions, or talk them over with a friend:

—Why is it that women always want men to wear belts?

—Why is it that women seem to like vegetables more than men do?

—Do you think there is some kind of evolutionary explanation for belts and vegetables? Like what?

—How does talking about relationships make you feel?

—How about answering the last question? How did that make you feel?

—Do you feel like you're more in touch with your feelings now? Why or why not?

—Think about that last question for a bit more. Is your answer different now? Are you sure?

Section VI:
Sex

OVERVIEW: *For many, sex is the whole reason for getting into a relationship with a member of the opposite sex. For others, it is an unpleasant obligation to be endured as infrequently as possible. Both are equally valid viewpoints. However, when each member of a relationship takes a different viewpoint, trouble can ensue. The following regulations apply whether a couple are seeing each other casually (POP) or have entered an exclusive relationship (MAD).*

A. Context of Romantic Activity

  i. **Wholesomeness.** Members of a MAD or POP relationship shall understand that

  a. Sex is an essential component of a romantic relationship.

  b. Sex is important for intimacy and a feeling of closeness and togetherness.

  c. The frequency or enthusiasm with which one indulges in sex in no way correlates negatively with moral character or good upbringing.

  ii. **Frequency.** Members shall strive to engage in sex frequently enough to satisfy their partners' innate erotic urges. The magnitude of sexual urges tends to decrease with age, such that members should have sex no less than

  a. Three times per week, if the youngest member of the couple is under twenty years of age

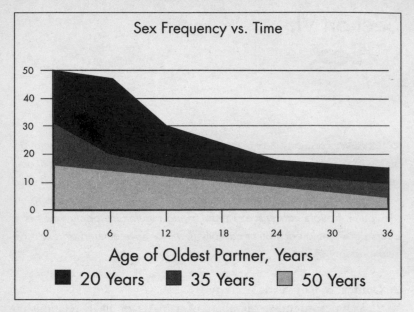

Fig. VI.1: Frequency of Sexual Intercourse as a Function of Relationship Duration. Cadres of 500 unmarried couples, whose eldest members were aged 19–21, 34–36, and 49–51, were polled at semiannual intervals as to the frequency of their sexual intercourse. As was expected, the youngest couples showed the highest frequency of sexual intercourse, and the eldest the least. All, however, showed significant decrease in sexual frequency as the relationships matured. Particularly interesting was a clearly defined turning point in the data corresponding to the "new booty hump," a colloquial term referring to the drastic drop-off in erotic fervor around the sixth month of a relationship. The effect was seen most clearly in the youngest demographic group, and less significantly in the thirty-five-year-old cadre. *Source: Proceedings of the American Sexological Institute*, Vol. CDXVII.

b. Twice per week, if the youngest member of the couple is between twenty and thirty years of age

c. Once per week, if the youngest member of the couple is between thirty and forty years of age

d. Twice per month, if the youngest member of the couple is between forty and fifty years of age

e. Once per month, if the youngest member of the couple is between fifty and sixty years of age

f. As required if the youngest member of the couple is over sixty years of age

iii. **Pressure for Sex**

1. Members of a POP relationship may inform their partners that they will not engage in sexual relations until after the establishment of a MAD. *(Note: However, see* UDR&B *Sec. IV.B.i.c.)*

2. Members of a dating relationship shall not pester, badger, or harrass their partners for sex.

3. Members shall be aware and understand that sexual appetite generally wanes after the first six to twelve months of a relationship *(note: see Fig. VI.1)* or after a partner has put on a good deal of weight.

B. **Foreplay**

i. **Definition**

a. **Duration.** Foreplay shall be understood to consist of that element of the erotic process extending from the first expression of sexual interest to initiation of penetrative intercourse.

b. **Purpose.** Foreplay shall be understood to comprise an essential step in the full romantic experience, serving to whet the sexual appetite so that the erotic expression might be performed as fully and fulfillingly as possible.

Stat Attack

Foreplay burns calories at a rate of 90 an hour, and sex a whopping 270 an hour. Turns out getting intimate is good for your heart in more ways than one!

Source: HomeArts.com.

   c. **Proper understanding.** Foreplay shall not be interpreted as a delaying tactic on the part of the female, or an unnecessary waste of time on the road to orgasm.

ii. **Initiation.** The following shall be understood to indicate that a partner is interested in initiating foreplay:

   a. Smoldering or sultry glances

   b. The licking of lips

   c. Naughty, ribald, or frisky wordplay

   d. Seductive body posture

   e. The grasping of a partner's body

iii. **Mood.** The following shall be understood to be conducive to the establishment of a proper mood:

   a. Scented candles

   b. Roaring fire

   c. Soft or sultry music

   d. The imbibing of alcoholic beverages

iv. **Acceptable Components.** The following are among the many acceptable components of foreplay:

   a. Kissing

   b. Stroking

   c. Hugging

   d. Caressing

  e. Massaging
  f. Whispering sweet nothings
  g. Removal of clothing
v. **Unacceptable Components.** The following shall not be deemed acceptable components of foreplay:
  a. Talking about money
  b. Watching a hockey game

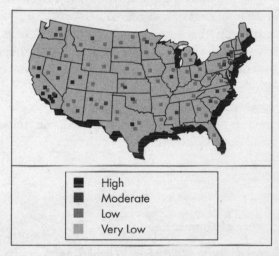

High
Moderate
Low
Very Low

Fig. VI.2. Average Length of Foreplay. Data from the 1998 Psychosociological Metasurvey were broken down by county and renormalized to show the average duration of foreplay as reported by unmarried couples between the ages of twenty-five and thirty-four. Areas in black show regions where length of average foreplay is high, in excess of twenty minutes per sexual episode. Areas in light gray represent regions where length of average foreplay is very low, less than thirty seconds. The state with the shortest average foreplay overall is Montana, with just forty-three seconds per episode. *Source:* "Let's Vigorous Life," *Japanese Ministry of Health and Discipline,* 1994.

c. Placing or taking a phone call

d. Arguing

vi. Duration

a. **Minimum.** Foreplay shall last no less than the amount of time required for both parties to become physically capable of engaging in intercourse.

b. **Maximum.** Foreplay shall last no longer than the amount of time by which either party becomes unable to restrain himself or herself from engaging in intercourse.

c. **Conflict.** If the time periods outlined in *UDR&B* Secs. VI.B.vi.a and b are mutually exclusive, then the more eager member of the couple shall be issued a warning and ordered to better restrain himself or herself.

d. **Time out.** If either or both parties shall become bored or lose interest before foreplay is completed, the romantic interlude shall come to an end.

Rule of Thumb

According to *UDR&B* Sec. VI.B.vii.a, partners who have been separated for "an excessively long period of time" may forgo foreplay prior to sex. How long is "excessively long"? It varies with age, among other things. Generally, partners who have been separated for twice the maximum interval between intercourse episodes *(note: see UDR&B Sec. VI.A.ii)* can skip the foreplay. That works out to four and two-thirds days for teenagers, and two months for fifty-to-sixty-year-olds.

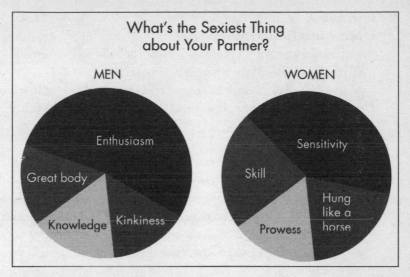

Fig. VI.3. Valuation Criteria in Sex Partner Selection. A random sample of 4,300 single Americans was surveyed by telephone regarding their sexual preferences. Wide disparities were seen in the relative ranking of sexual selection criteria between males and females. A large plurality of men cited "enthusiasm" as their favorite aspect of their partners' sexuality, while a smaller plurality of women chose "sensitivity," with "hung like a horse" behind by a narrow margin. Evidently, sexual performance is considered by many Americans to be an important aspect of the erotic experience. *Source: My First Big Book of Psychosexual Socioanthropology,* University of Chicago Press, 1999.

vii. **Exceptions.** Partners may skip foreplay if
    a. They have been separated for an excessively long period of time.
    b. They are under the age of nineteen.
    c. They are drunk.

C. Intercourse

i. Miminum Requirements

a. Persons engaged in sexual relations shall attempt to provide as much pleasure to their partners as possible.

b. Persons shall attempt to enjoy themselves and not view sex as a chore, burden, or obligation to be dispensed with as quickly as possible.

ii. Contraceptives

a. Each party shall undertake to ensure independently that proper birth control methods are taken.

b. If a couple has been sleeping together for less than two weeks, or has not progressed beyond the POP phase of the relationship, the male shall in any case wear a condom.

c. The following shall be understood not to constitute acceptable birth control:

1. Rhythm method
2. Pulling out early
3. Trusting in fate

iii. Experimentation

a. Partners shall

1. Be aware that exploration is a healthy part of a mature sexual experience
2. Attempt to keep an open mind on the subject of sexually novel positions, gadgets, techniques, or ideas

b. Partners shall not

1. Denigrate, ridicule, or sneer at a partner's suggestion to try something new
2. Force a partner to try something he or she clearly does not want to do
3. Attempt to involve third parties in the sexual act

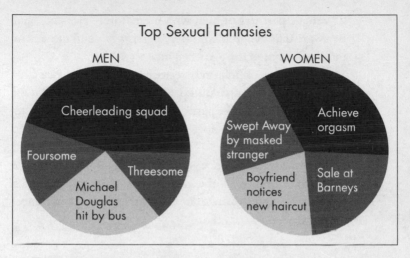

Fig. VI.4. Top Sexual Fantasies. Male and female readers of a popular general-interest magazine were invited to mail in brief descriptions of their favorite visualizations used during intercourse. The majority of male respondents favored scenarios in which they engaged in sexual relations with multiple partners simultaneously. Female respondents skewed more heavily toward sensuous pleasures, attention from their partners, and the hope of someday being able to achieve orgasm. *Source:* "Get It Hot, Get It Heavy," *Reader's Digest* magazine, July 1997.

    4. Spring unusual or bizarre sexual practices without explicit mutual agreement and enthusiasm, particularly early in the relationship

iv. **Dysfunction**

  a. **Premature ejaculation**

    1. **Definition.** Ejaculation is deemed to have occurred prematurely if the male achieves orgasm within two minutes of penetration, or at any time before his partner has succeeded in fully removing her clothes.

2. Female partners of men who prematurely ejaculate shall be aware that the problem rarely persists beyond the second interlude, or after the age of eighteen.

3. Males who prematurely ejaculate shall be aware that women rarely go on second dates with men who exhibit the problem, and shall take particular pains to show gratitude toward any woman who does.

b. **Impotence**

1. **Definition.** Impotence is the failure of a man to attain or maintain turgidity of the penis. Its three most common causes are fatigue, drunkenness, and the presence of camera crews.

Clip out this box, laminate it, and keep it in your wallet, handbag, or purse for handy reference.

Hello. If you're reading this card, it's probably because your partner is exhibiting a temporary sexual dysfunction and wishes to ease your mind. Please be assured that occasional penile flaccidity or vaginal dryness is a common occurrence, and in no way reflects upon your partner's sexuality, secret gender orientation, or the extent to which he or she finds you attractive. Please remain calm, treat your partner with sympathy and support, and we're sure that in no time you and your partner will be up and running with all systems "go"!

Sincerely,
American Dating Association
Department of Education and Outreach

2. A single instance of impotence shall not be interpreted by a female as a sign that her partner does not find her attractive.

3. The partner of a male exhibiting impotence shall not mock, berate, or ridicule him.

4. Persistent impotence may require medical assistance, or may be a sign that member does not find partner attractive, or that he is gay.

c. **Coitus interruptus**

1. **Definition.** Coitus interruptus is sexual intercourse that fails to reach a timely and satisfactory conclusion because it is in some way disturbed or interrupted.

2. Partners experiencing coitus interruptus shall understand that in order for intercourse to resume they may need to start from scratch, arousal-wise.

3. If a couple is currently engaged in penetrative intercourse neither party shall disrupt the proceedings for the sake of non-life-threatening reasons, such as to answer the telephone, put coins in a parking meter, take the laundry out of the dryer, or catch the beginning of *Days of Our Lives*.

v. **Forbidden Behavior**

a. **Attempts to initiate sex.** No person shall attempt to initiate sexual intercourse after his or her partner has already fallen asleep.

b. **Incorrect name.** No person shall address his or her partner by someone else's name.

c. **Inappropriate exclamations.** No person shall shout "What's my name?" or "Who's your daddy?" during intercourse.

d. **Excessive exuberance.** No person shall shout, scream, bang walls, or otherwise create noise to such an extent as to invite the notice and/or censure of the neighbors.

e. **Distasteful behavior.** No person shall persist in any erotic activities which clearly cause revulsion, alarm, or despair in his or her partner.

D. **Interpreting Partner's Response**

i. **Communication**

a. Persons engaging in sexual relations shall attempt to convey, through touch or speech, what is and is not working to increase their arousal, and what they would like their partners to do.

b. A person shall make every effort to decipher what is causing pleasure or pain in his or her partner, and what he or she desires to be done.

c. All persons shall understand that a partner who says "no" shall be understood to mean it, and that all further erotic activity must cease, unless said word "no" is accompanied by obvious displays of continuing passion.

ii. **Evidence of Heightened Arousal.** The following shall be taken as evidence that a person's partner is experiencing heightened levels of sexual arousal:

a. A flushed appearance of the skin

b. Engorgement of the nipples and genitals

c. Lubrication of the vaginal membrane

d. Sweating

e. Moaning

f. Grasping, clutching, or scratching

g. Biting

h. Screaming

i. Writhing

(Note: The latter five of these indications are also associated with pain. When in doubt, a person engaging in sexual intercourse shall clarify the matter promptly with his or her partner.)

Dating Tip

If your partner closes his or her eyes or looks away while approaching climax, it's because he or she is fantasizing about someone else.

iii. **Evidence of Declining Arousal.** The following shall be taken as evidence that a person's partner is experiencing decreasing levels of sexual arousal:

  a. Skin is cool and dry

  b. Body motion decreases

  c. Flaccidity or detumescence of genitals

  d. Dryness of vagina

  e. Sighs, yawning, or snores

  f. Partner puts on clothes

E. **Climax**

  i. **Male**

    a. **Failure to achieve.** If a male should fail to achieve orgasm, the sexual interlude shall necessarily be deemed unsuccessful.

    b. **Postorgasmic buffer period.** A female shall not attempt to reinitiate sexual relations for at least twenty minutes after her male partner has achieved orgasm.

    c. **Maximal intensity levels.** No male shall be expected by his partner to perform intercourse more than

      1. Four (4) times per twenty-four hours, if he is less than twenty years of age

      2. Three (3) times per twenty-four hours, if he is twenty or more but less than thirty years of age

3. Two (2) times per twenty-four hours, if he is thirty or more but less than forty years of age

4. One (1) time per twenty-four hours, if he is over forty years of age

d. If a male does not achieve orgasm within thirty minutes, his female partner may request that the sexual interlude be terminated immediately.

ii. **Female**

a. No female engaged in sexual relations with her partner shall fake an orgasm.

b. Every male engaged in sexual relations shall make every due effort to ensure that his female partner achieves orgasm.

1. However, sex shall not be deemed a failure if a female partner does not achieve orgasm.

2. If a female achieves multiple orgasm during sexual intercourse she shall compliment her male partner upon this fact.

iii. **Exclamations.** No person shall utter weird, disturbing, or silly exclamations upon achieving climax, including but not limited to

a. There you go!

b. Shazam!

c. Heeeere's Johnny!

d. Pardon me, miss.

e. Hello, Cincinnati!

F. **Aftermath**

i. **Postcoital Contact**

a. A person shall attempt not to fall asleep immediately upon achieving orgasm, particularly if his or her partner is still attempting to achieve same.

b. Upon mutual completion of sexual relations, persons shall remain awake and physically in contact for a period of no less than five (5) minutes. Persons shall under no circumstances run to the bathroom and immediately and ostentatiously gargle.

> **Dating Haiku**
> **"Faith and Flesh"**
>
> Two souls are melding
> Spirits fuse and push, pulsing.
> Neighbors bang on wall
>
> —G. Laurencia Bigelow,
> *Mad Drunk with Cordite*,
> Firelight Publishing,
> Seattle, 1993

c. It is no longer universally acceptable to smoke in bed after sex. Persons may smoke if

1. Partner permits it
2. Terms of apartment lease and/or municipal code do not prohibit it.

d. After the minimum period of postcoital contact has expired *(note: see* UDR&B *Sec. VI.F.i.b, above)*, partners shall be free to

1. Fall asleep
2. Turn on the television
3. Take a call

ii. **Discretion After the Fact**

a. While a relationship is still in effect no person shall reveal the intimate details of its sexual relations to:

1. Friends
2. Colleagues
3. Family members
4. Radio call-in shows
5. Daytime talk show audiences
6. Any other person, with exception of priests, rabbis, therapists, and licensed physicians

G. Other Issues
i. Masturbation
a. Persons engaged in sexual relationships shall understand that masturbation is a healthy expression of a person's sexual energies.

A Closer Look: Is My Boyfriend a Perv?

According to a recent survey, 43 percent of all women believe that their boyfriends are perverts. While this may be a widespread perception, it is probably not accurate. Paraphiliacs, as they are know in technical terms, are defined by psychologists as persons depending on, for sexual arousal, ideas, images, or practices so far beyond the norms of society as to subject themselves to ridicule or contempt. As defined in these terms, only an estimated 2 to 3 percent of the population qualify as paraphiliacs. Among the stranger paraphilias:

Acrotomophilia—Arousal by fantasizing about having sex with an amputee
Apotemnophilia—Arousal by fantasizing about becoming an amputee
Crush fetish—Arousal by the squashing to death or crushing of small animals
Eproctophilia—Arousal by flatulence
Giantess fetish—Erotic fascination with imaginary women more than one hundred feet tall
Symphorophilia—Arousal by fantasies of arranging a crash or explosion
Tripsolagnia—Arousal from having hair shampooed

So if your partner is only fantasizing about chaining you up and smearing you with motor oil, perhaps you should count your blessings.

---

b. No person shall be berated, criticized, or censured for masturbating, nor shall any person attempt to force or compel another not to masturbate.

c. No person shall leave used tissues, dirty magazines, lubricants, vibrators, or other evidence of his or her masturbation lying around for others to stumble upon.

d. No person shall masturbate with such frequency or vehemence that he or she is unable to perform his or her sexual duties with his or her partner.

ii. **Safari Sex**

a. Persons engaged in a sexual relationship may undertake, for the sake of variety and increased excitement, to have sex in novel or unusual settings or situations, such as

　1. Outdoors, for instance at the beach or on a mountaintop

　2. In an airplane lavatory

　3. In a moving car

b. Persons engaged in safari sex shall remain aware of potential environmental hazards, such as

　1. The delubricating effects of water, sand, etc.

　2. Cuts, abrasions, and bruises inflicted by harsh natural settings

　3. In-flight turbulence

　4. Any other possible or likely eventuality which may lead to death, injury, or coitus interruptus *(note: see* UDR&B *Sec. VI.C.iv.c, above)*

c. Persons shall take pains to avoid discovery by unwitting third parties.

d. Persons shall be aware that lewd conduct is a misdemeanor offense in all fifty states and is subject to a fine and/or imprisonment.

Discussion Points

After reading carefully through Section VI, think about the following questions, or talk them over with friends:

— Women can have multiple orgasms, but men can have orgasms whenever they want. Who do you think is better off?
— Men: Would you sleep with that fat woman from *The Drew Carey Show* if you got to sleep with Catherine Zeta-Jones right afterward? Women: Would you sleep with the Elephant Man if right afterward you got to sleep with that actor who was on the cover of *Vanity Fair* two years ago and was supposed to become huge but never did?
— Sometimes when people are trying to be hyperbolic about something they'll say it's "better than sex." Do you think that's ever really possible?
— Which is more disturbing, teenagers having sex or really old people having sex?
— Do you think this book would have sold better if all the chapters had been about sex instead of just one?

iii. **Phone Sex**
   a. **Definition.** Phone sex shall be understood to consist of simultaneous masturbation between two remote parties engaged in lewd talk over the telephone.
   b. **Moral equivalence.** Phone sex shall be deemed morally equivalent to actual sex for the purposes of
      1. Maintaining minimum acceptable levels of sexual frequency while a person is far away from his or her partner
      2. Determining whether a person is guilty of infidelity

Section VII:
Moving In

OVERVIEW: *The great American sage Benjamin Franklin put it best: "Two moves equals a fire." Of all the great stepping stones of a relationship, none—apart from getting married, of course—is as fraught with emotional tension, misunderstanding, aggravation, and potential for disaster as the act of moving in. On the other hand, it is also a time when two people who care a great deal for each other are able to show their feelings in a direct, hands-on way. If everyone behaves properly, according to the strictures of society's rules, then the chances are good that moving in will be an experience that both parties in a relationship will later look back on with fondness.*

A. Initiation
i. **Eligibility.** Persons shall not move in with their partners, or agree to have their partners move in with them, unless

a. They have already entered into a Mutually Agreed State of Dating (MAD). *(Note: See* UDR&B *Sec. V, "Advanced Courtship.")*

b. They have already told their partners that they love them.

c. Their partners have already told them that they love them also.

d. Each member of the MAD relationship feels confident that he or she will in all likelihood continue to date his or her partner for at least another year, or for the duration of the shared lease, whichever is greater.

e. Each member of the MAD has introduced his or her parents

to his or her partner, unless he or she intends never to do so, even in the event of marriage.

f. Each member of the relationship has the means and the willingness to pay half of the monthly cost of the habitation. *(Note: However, see* UDR&B *Sec. VIII.C.ii.c.)*

g. Neither member has unduly pressured, threatened, or blackmailed the other into undertaking said move.

h. He or she is impelled by at least one of the following valid motivations:

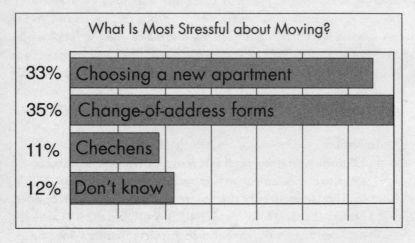

Fig. VII.1. Prime Moving-Related Stress Factors. One thousand unmarried American couples who had moved in together within the last forty-eight months were polled by telephone and asked what factor had caused them the greatest amount of psychological stress immediately prior to or during their move. Two categories, "Choosing a new apartment" and "Change-of-address forms," received the greatest portion of affirmative responses, while fear of Chechen mafiosi garnered relatively few responses. *Source: Terror from Grozny: The Lurking Peril of Caucasian Gangsterism,* Komsomolsk Press, 1998.

    1. Genuine desire to share daily life with partner.

    2. Partner has much nicer apartment.

    3. Parents started charging rent.

    4. Current roommate is loathsome due to slovenliness, foul manners, or general personality disfunction.

ii. **By Invitation**

a. A party may move into the home or lodging of his or her partner upon explicit invitation.

b. Such invitation must be made while the inviter is sober, or, if made while intoxicated, must be reconfirmed later when the inviter is once more sober.

c. An invitation to a partner to move in, once made, may not be retracted prior to the move-in. *(Note: See* UDR&B *Sec. V.A.v.c, "Irreversibility.")*

iii. **By Fait Accompli.** If a party shall have transferred eight out of the following ten items into a partner's habitation, and not received an objection thereupon from said partner after a period of not less than two (2) weeks, then the act of moving in shall be deemed to have occurred by a process of fait accompli:

a. Toothbrush

b. Diaphragm

c. Teddy bear

d. Pajamas

e. At least two (2) feet of books on bookshelf

f. Armoire, bureau, chest of drawers, or entertainment center

g. At least five (5) items of clothing necessary for season not currently under way, such as a ski ensemble in July

h. At least three (3) houseplants of no less than five (5) pounds gross weight each

i. A dog or cat

    j. A band saw, grand piano, or rotating shoe tree

B. **Relocation and Transport**

  i. **Moving**

    a. Each partner will assist in the moving to the full extent of his or her ability.

    b. It is understood that the man will do most of the heavy lifting, regardless of his physical condition.

    c. A woman may request that large objects such as sofas, refrigerators, and book shelving be put in specific locations, but once they are in place, she may not change her mind.

    d. If a couple choose to hire professional movers, they shall split the cost evenly.

    e. If a man invites a group of his friends to assist in the move, they may not spend more time drinking than working until such time as the move has been accomplished.

    f. Neither party may elect to move

      1. Home gym equipment that has not been used in more than eighteen (18) months except as a clothes hanger

      2. Computers more than two (2) years old

      3. Clothes that have not been worn in more than two years, except occasional clothing such as tuxedos, ball gowns, and Halloween costumes

      4. Jars or cartons of perishable food items whose provenance is so antique as to predate memory

      5. Any other possessions that are inherently heavy, worthless, and/or dangerous

C. **Unpacking and Decoration**

  i. **Unpacking**

    a. **Duplicate items.** If consolidated households have duplicate items, e.g., stereos, televisions, then

    1. One item will be left in the hands of friends or relatives for safekeeping until such time as a breakup may occur, or

    2. Room shall be found for both, or

    3. One shall be disposed of, and its owner shall be prepared to suffer its loss in the event of a breakup

  b. **Storage space**

    1. The member of the relationship who originally occupied the house or apartment in question shall clear a reasonable amount of closet, bureau, and other storage space.

    2. If it is necessary to purchase additional bureaus, dressers, and other storage equipment, both parties shall share the cost equally.

    3. No partner shall intentionally "lose," "misplace" or cause to be stolen his or her partner's belongings merely for the sake of creating more storage space for his or her own self.

  c. **Preservation of privacy.** The fact that a person may, in the course of moving his or her partner's belongings, find himself or herself carrying a box or carton of his or her partner's private letters or documents does not in any way entitle said person to rifle through them.

ii. **Decoration**

  a. **Aesthetic decisions**

    1. Both parties shall have some input into the scope, style, and details of any planned decoration of the shared habitation.

    2. It shall be understood that the female member of the relationship shall have greater deci-

---

**Dating Haiku:
"Moving Day"**

Styrofoam nuggets
Crumpled newspaper, boxes
Somewhere, a cat mews.

—G. Laurencia Bigelow,
Songs in the Key of Me,
Firelight Publishing,
Seattle, 1993

sion-making power than her partner on issues of scope, style, and details of planned redecoration.

3. A man shall not complain unduly about the scope, style, or details of any effected decoration.

b. **Labor**

1. Each party shall assist in the labor of decoration, including hammering, sawing, wallpapering, and painting, to the best of his or her ability.

2. It shall be expected that the male member of a relationship will do most of the labor required in decorating.

A Closer Look: Pets

Dogs, cats, and other household pets are more than just good friends and loyal companions. They are also unpredictable time bombs of potential violence, vectors for potentially lethal diseases, and a seed bed for relationship conflict. Before getting emotionally attached to a pet owner, take the time to learn what hidden dangers your partner's pet may harbor.

Dogs: biting, scratching, pooing, peeing, allergies
Cats: biting, scratching, pooing, peeing, allergies, suffocating babies
Fish: existential woe
Birds: irritation
Snakes: creepiness, bites, full or partial ingestion of owner or guests
Ferrets: rabies, climbing up trouser legs

Source: Animals, Animals, Animals! Golden Book Press, 1995.

Discussion Points

After reading carefully through Section VII, think about the following questions, or talk them over with a friend:

—Have you ever moved in with somebody? What was the hardest part about it?

—Do you think that too much intimacy can actually kill romance?

—Do you think that if a person has a bad or crazy pet, that it reflects badly on them? On their future parenting skills?

—Do you think it's possible that a person's pet could just "disappear" one day? How hard would it be?

—What if it turned out that you were somehow involved? Would that put the kibosh on the relationship?

—Would it be worth the risk anyway?

3. No person shall complain about the quality of decorating work if he or she has not helped in its execution.

4. No decision on paint color may be reversed once the first dab of paint has touched the wall.

D. Residential Rights

i. Equality

a. If one partner is moving into another's existing house or apartment, he or she shall not be made to feel as a permanent guest, but as a full-fledged co-householder, with all concomitant rights and responsibilities.

    b. Once the move has been accomplished, neither party shall be made to feel he or she is a burden or an imposition on the other.

ii. **Pets**

    a. **Grandfather clause.** The act of moving in shall not be grounds for either party to make hints that it is time for his or her partner's pet to be

1. Given away
2. Put to sleep
3. Set free
4. "Lost"
5. In any way disposed of

Section VIII:
Living Together

OVERVIEW: *A shared home can be a zone of comfort in which romance, passion, intellect, and togetherness all play out on a daily stage. It can also be the ultimate test of two people's fitness to remain together as a couple.*

Truly, there is no better way to get to know someone than to witness their behavior day in, day out, as the seasons roll by and one year blends into the next. How does a person respond when the neighbor's dog digs up the flower bed for the fourteenth time? How does he or she take care of a partner who comes down with a sudden, nasty case of the flu?

Statistics show that after four years, only 30 percent of all cohabiting couples will still be living together—but that of these, fully two-thirds will be doing so as a married couple.

A. Housekeeping
i. Level of Housekeeping

a. Both members of a household shall strive to maintain a level of hygiene and orderliness commensurate with the predilections of the more fastidious member.

b. Given that the general trend of human civilization and society is toward increasing hygiene and orderliness, the more fastidious member of the cohabiting couple shall undertake in a patient and understanding manner the education of the less fastidious member in the ways of cleanliness and good order.

c. Provided that the less fastidious member makes a good-faith effort to maintain an acceptable level of housekeeping, his or her partner shall not excessively berate, criticize, or bemoan his or her messiness.

ii. **Responsibility**

a. Parties shall be responsible for the cleaning up of messes which they create.

b. No party shall be held accountable for the maintenance or cleaning of any particular arena of housekeeping simply by the fact of their gender, as for instance

1. The raking of leaves
2. The ironing of laundry
3. The cleaning of gutters
4. The taking out of garbage

c. In general, all household chores shall be shared equally by both members of a cohabiting couple.

d. If a couple decide that one member of the relationship shall undertake responsibility for a particular arena of housekeeping, the other will undertake responsibility for an arena or arenas of commensurate laboriousness. *(Note: The issue of whether or not a person may actually enjoy his or her chores shall not be factored into the apportioning thereof.)*

e. Sexual acts shall not be regarded as chores.

 Rule of Thumb: Housekeeping

If each member of a couple feels that they are doing two-thirds of the housework, then the housework is being split evenly.

iii. Bathroom

a. Toilet seats

1. Toilet seats shall be raised before a man commences micturition.

2. Toilet seat shall be lowered immediately thereafter.

3. Toilets seats shall be left lowered at all other times, barring some immediate and temporary need.

b. Cremes, salves, and emollients.

A woman shall be permitted to store no more than the following number of items in a shared bathroom:

1. Bottles of moisturizer: six (6)

2. Bottles of conditioner: eight (8)

3. Bottles of shampoo: ten (10)

4. Other bottles of lotions, cremes, emollients, and any other such liquids: eighteen (18)

iv. Kitchen

a. Cooking

1. Neither member of a cohabiting couple shall cook, prepare, or otherwise present food for joint consumption that he or she knows the other party to find unpalatable.

2. Neither member of a couple shall criticize the other's cooking, unless he or she is prepared to do the cooking himself or herself.

3. Domino's pizza shall not be ordered more than four (4) times per week.

**Dating Haiku
"The Laundry Machine"**

Socks mixed, his and hers
Warm lovely scent of
laundry soap
Everything is pink

—G. Laurencia Bigelow,
Dance of the Anemone,
Firelight Publishing,
Seattle, 1994

Stat Attack

Sixty-two percent of all single people who travel regularly as part of their job have had a one-night stand while on a business trip. *Source:* Alliance of American Statisticians.

B. External Relations
i. Attitude and Demeanor

a. Members of a cohabiting couple shall not act as though they are married and hence become boring.

b. Each shall earnestly endeavor to do as many fun things as possible in life, and to include the other person in amusing, entertaining, and exciting activities, such as

1. **Music and dancing.** Members of a cohabiting couple shall strive to keep current with musical trends, and to enjoy the sensuous pleasures of the dance with one another.

2. **Eating out.** Members of a cohabiting couple shall endeavor to eat out at least once per week. *(Note: Driving to KFC, getting takeout, and watching a video at home shall not be deemed "eating out.")*

3. **Travel.** Neither member may go to a tropical island, ski getaway, or similarly luxurious and appealing destination without bringing along his or her partner, or, failing that, at least inviting him or her in a sincere manner.

ii. Socializing
a. Third-party friendships

1. Members of a cohabiting couple shall not discourage partners from maintaining friendships, but rather shall strive to always extend warm welcomes to said friends, inquire

after their well-being, and in general make them feel appreciated and wanted.

2. Either member shall be free to go out and see friends on his or her own, whenever he or she wants, without receiving a hassle from his or her partner, so long as all such friendships are fully compliant. *(Note: See* UDR&B *Sec. V.B.iii.b., "Platonic friendships.")*

b. **Evenings out**

1. **Coming home late.** If socializing without his or her partner, a member shall come home no later than 11 P.M. on a weeknight, or 1 A.M. on a weekend.

2. **Coming home drunk.** Neither member shall come home excessively drunk or intoxicated, especially on a frequent basis.

3. **Reporting in.** Neither party shall be obliged, when out socializing without his or her partner, to continuously call in to report his or her location and activities

4. Upon returning from socializing with friends, members shall give an honest accounting of what they did, where, and with whom.

iii. **House Guests**

a. **Visits from friends**

1. No member of a cohabiting couple shall vehemently protest a visit by a partner's friend.

2. No member shall permit excessively long visits by his or her friends.

3. No member shall permit any visits by irritating, depressing, insane, larcenous, foul-smelling, or infectious friends.

4. Friends shall not criticize partners while under the same roof.

5. No member shall complain about a partner's visiting friend while in said friend's presence.

b. **Visits from family**

1. A member of a cohabiting couple shall warmly welcome any and all overnight visits from a partner's family.

2. No member shall seek out, agree to, or otherwise endorse excessively long or frequent visits from family members.

3. Members are entitled to continue sharing the same bed during visits from family members.

4. Family members shall not criticize, berate, belittle, or bemoan a partner while under the same roof, nor shall they urge, plot, plan, or otherwise endorse the dissolution of the relationship.

A Closer Look: How Long Is Too Long?

The *UDR&B* specifies that family members' visits shall not be "excessively long." The regulation has been left deliberately vague so as to allow for variations in local custom, time of year, the degree to which the family members are unsanitary or crude, and other such variables. However, as a general guideline, any of the following may be taken as indicators that family guests may have overstayed their welcome:

— You've had to mow the lawn twice since they showed up.
— They have memorized all the channels on your cable system.
— They get angry if you sit on their favorite spot on the sofa.
— They get mail delivered at your house.

c. **Visits from exes.** Neither member of a cohabiting couple shall seek out, encourage, agree to, or otherwise endorse overnight visits from exes. No exceptions shall be made, regardless of the fact that the ex in question is reputedly

1. "So over me."
2. "So not like that."
3. Gay.

C. Money

i. Finances

a. **Fiduciary responsibility.** Each member shall strive to diligently protect, uphold, and maintain the integrity of the household finances.

1. Neither member shall steal from the other.
2. Neither member shall defraud the other, as by exaggerating or fabricating expenses, by misappropriating funds, or by mischaracterizing purchases.
3. Neither shall spend lavishly on items to be paid for out of the common budget.
4. Neither party shall buy Internet stocks on margin.

ii. Expenses

a. **Bills.** All bills and household expenses shall be split evenly, unless one person uses the service or product more than 80 percent of the time, in which case that person shall pay for all of it.

b. **Going out.** Though male and female members will split most expenses evenly, the male member will occasionally treat his partner to dinner, drinks, and other forms of entertainment and leisure.

c. **Dependency.** If one member of a cohabiting couple is unable to afford the expenses associated with joint residence, he or

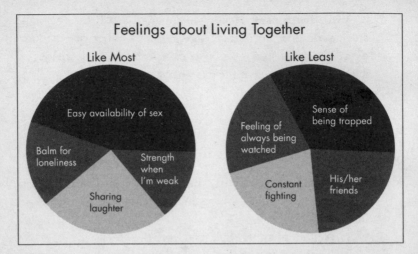

Fig.VIII.1. What Do You Like/Dislike Most About Living Together? A survey of 1,300 single cohabiters living in the southeastern United States was polled by telephone as to their most and least favorite aspects of living with their mates. Most respondents cited the easy availability of sex as the prime advantage of cohabitation, while the sense of being trapped was rated its biggest drawback. *Source:* Bell, D., and Perkins, R., "Psychosociological Responses to Premarital Cohabitation," *Journal of Domestic Science,* Vol. CDII.

she may be deemed dependent on the other. If both parties are amenable to this state of dependence, then rules *UDR&B* VIII.C.ii.a and b above may be waived. A person shall only be permitted to seek dependent status if he or she is at least two of the following:

1. A good deal more good-looking than his or her partner
2. Not particularly smart, energetic, or ambitious
3. An actor

D. Domestic Conduct
i. Nocturnal Habits
a. Snoring
1. Members awakened or kept awake by a partner's snoring may poke or prod them until such time as said snoring ceases.

 **ADA Case Study**

In May 1993, twenty-nine-year-old John Harvey rose at 4 A.M. from the bed he shared with twenty-six-year-old Ellen Fairbanks to go to the bathroom. Barely awake, he stumbled through the darkness to the bathroom, micturated, and groggily returned to the bed. However, just as he was about to slide back into his warm spot, Ms. Fairbanks roused herself from slumber long enough to ask him to get a glass of water. Mr. Harvey flatly refused, got back into bed, and was soon fast asleep.

The incident was all but forgotten until two months later, when, in the heat of an acrimonious breakup, Ms. Fairbanks cited the evening's events as evidence of Mr. Harvey's noncompliant tendencies. Mr. Harvey counter-argued that since he was returning to bed, not leaving it, he had been under no obligation to fetch her water.

Such was the bitterness of the breakup that Mr. Harvey went so far as to bring the matter before the ADA Arbitration Board. Alas for Mr. Harvey, the board ruled against him, deciding in a 3–2 judgment that the wording of *UDR&B* Sec. VIII.D.i.b meant that any member of a cohabiting couple who was out of the bed was obligated to fetch water on request, whether they were coming or going.

Interesting Fact

The average male's body temperature is 5 degrees warmer than the female's. Scientifically, it's impossible for both in a couple to be comfortable at the same thermostat setting with the same set of bedding.

    2. Members shall recognize that snoring is an involuntary behavior, and not criticize, complain, or harass their partners about it.

b. **Drink of water.** Any member who gets out of bed for any reason in the middle of the night shall get his or her partner a glass of water if requested to do so.

c. **Side of bed**

    1. Whoever owns the bed shall decide which side he or she wants to sleep on.

    2. If the bed is new, then the original inhabitant of the shared habitation shall choose which side he or she wishes to sleep on.

    3. If both the bed and the habitation are new, then the woman shall be permitted to choose which side she wishes to sleep on.

    4. No person shall whimsically and suddenly decide to sleep on the other side of the bed without his or her partner's willing assent.

    5. When traveling or staying overnight in places other than their own home, members shall sleep on their usual sides of the bed, except by mutual agreement to the contrary.

    6. Persons shall not be forced to sleep in areas which have become saturated with moisture for whatever reason.

    d. **Hogging.** No person shall hog

      1. Pillows

      2. Sheets

      3. Blanket, duvet, or comforter

    e. **Pets.** Pets shall under no circumstances be permitted to sleep on or in the bed, unless both partners explicitly assent.

ii. **Personal Space**

    a. **Personal space.** Space permitting, each member is entitled to retain a portion of the shared habitation exclusively for his or her own use, to be utilized as workshop, office, playroom, storage area, or any other function necessary for his or her desired pursuit, so long as said pursuit is compliant with accepted dating practices.

    b. **Invasion.** Personal space shall not be invaded, probed, or explored by the other member without his or her partner's explicit prior invitation.

iii. **Television Viewing**

    a. **Control of remote.** Use of the remote control should be shared equally and fairly between members of a cohabiting relationship.

    b. **Choice of channel.** Whichever member has the remote shall be deemed the ultimate arbiter of what shall be watched at that moment.

    c. **Relinquishment of control.** Any person who leaves the room to go to the bathroom, fetch a snack, etc., shall be deemed to have ceded control of the remote.

    d. **Voicing objections.** The member not in control of the remote may voice opinions about his or her partner's choice of programming, but not excessively so as to interfere with viewing enjoyment.

Trivia Corner

Taking care of pets can be a lot like raising children. But not in every way, fortunately. According to Census Bureau statistics, keeping pets can increase an owner's lifespan by three to five years. But raising children reduces each parent's lifespan by an average of eighteen months per child!

Source: U.S. Census Bureau.

    e. **Forbidden programming.** When both members of a couple are in the same room and actively watching the television, the following programs may not be selected by the member in charge of the remote:

    1. Professional wrestling
    2. Bass fishing tournaments
    3. Home shopping
    4. Shows in which women cry, hug, or "share"

E. **Joint Responsibilities**
  i. **Pets**
    a. **Acquired pets**
    1. Once members of a couple have begun living together, neither shall obtain a pet of any description without the explicit, sober, nonpestered approval of his or her partner.
    2. Pets acquired after a couple have begun living together shall be cared for and fed jointly and equally by both members.

    b. **Surrogate child-rearing**
    1. Both members of a cohabiting couple shall understand that acquiring a pet after moving in together will cause their friends to make comments to the effect that they are likely practicing for having children, and not complain.

2. Should members actually desire to practice their future parenting skills, or to test a partner's potential parenting skills, they shall be aware that the following animals are not suitable for this purpose: badgers; bats; cattle; cougars; crocodiles; dingos; dolphins; eels; feral pigs; fish; gazelles; geese; great apes; hyenas; lizards; monkeys; naked mole rats; raccoons; rats; sharks; sloths; tapirs; tarantulas; turkeys; wildebeests; wolves; and any snakes that eat live animals and grow to more than six feet in length.

Discussion Points

After reading carefully through Section VIII, think about the following questions, or talk them over with a friend:

—On the whole, who do you think tends to be neater, men or women?

—Was your answer to the last question sexist?

—What's the most revolting thing you've ever seen in a bathroom? Was it *your* bathroom?

—Which would be worse, to have your partner's parents walk in on you while you are having sex, or to walk in on them while they're having sex?

—The French writer J. P. Sartre once wrote a play in which a man and a woman were trapped in a room together forever. By the end of the play they realize that they are in hell. Do you think that living together can be like that?

Section IX:
Termination

OVERVIEW: *All good things must come to an end. The great circle of life is forever turning, bringing the new into the world, carrying away the aged, and generally keeping things in motion. Time waits for no man, and certainly not for daters.*

Dating is an inherently transient form of relationship—and it is becoming more so. In 1980, the average dating relationship lasted 1.7 years. By 1995, that figure had fallen to just 1.5 years. On the bright side, the percentage of couples who exited dating for engagement or marriage rose from 1.5 to 2.3 percent.

As the band Semisonic puts it in their song "Closing Time," ". . . every new beginning comes from some other beginning's end." Even if it results not in marriage but in solitude and loneliness, the end of dating need not be a time of sadness, for within it lie the seeds of another bright new tomorrow.

A. **General**

i. **Definition.** "Termination" shall be understood to include any process by which a dating relationship comes to an end, including

a. **Breakup.** Any process by which a MAD relationship is intentionally nullified, to the joint knowledge of both participants, shall be termed "breaking up."

1. A breakup shall not be deemed to have occurred unless both parties are aware that the relationship has been dissolved.

ADA Case Study

In 1987, while visiting friends at the University of Virginia, nineteen-year-old Benjamin Shade became intoxicated by drinking beer and met up with an eighteen-year-old frosh, Marjorie Splint. He told her that he had just broken up with his girlfriend, nineteen-year-old Vanessa Maddock, a fellow student at Princeton. Shade subsequently succeeded in achieving intercourse with Splint.

The following morning, Maddock called the dorm room where Shade was staying, and a ten-minute conversation ensued, which Splint could easily overhear, and in which no mention of a breakup was made. Splint filed a Rogue Dater petition with the ADA, claiming that Shade had violated *UDR&B* Sec. II.B.iii.a.1, which calls for full disclosure of dating status during initial meeting. In his defense, Shade counterargued that he had already made up his mind that he would break up with Maddock as soon as he got back to school, so the relationship was effectively over. The Arbitration Board ruled unanimously that Shade was noncompliant, as no breakup can be considered to be in effect until both parties are aware of its existence.

Interestingly, observers have often pointed out that had Shade adopted a different defense—that he and Maddock had not yet arrived at exclusivity—his chances would have been far better. Indeed, his case is often cited as an example of why it is always desirable to obtain counsel before undergoing arbitration proceedings.

2. The breakup shall be deemed to be in effect from the moment either party has voiced a desire for the relationship to be dissolved.

3. Parties do not need to agree on the wisdom or desirability of said breakup in order for it to be in effect.

4. The person initiating the breakup shall be referred to as the "breaker."

5. The person not initiating the breakup shall be referred to as the "breakee."

b. **Engagement.** If members of a MAD relationship become engaged to be married, their MAD status shall be deemed to have come to an end.

c. **Marriage.** If members of a MAD relationship become married with or without passing through a prior period of engagement, their MAD status shall be deemed to have come to an end.

d. **Death or permanent disappearance.** If a person vanishes or ceases to exist, his or her partner is deemed free of all obligations and duties formerly undertaken as a member of a dating relationship.

Stat Attack

Considering marriage? Studies show that a life of happy marriage can increase a woman's life span by as much as 13 percent, and a man's as much as 2 percent. On the other hand, 77 percent of couples married three years or more report a "significant drop" in the frequency and quality of their sex lives, and 49 percent file for divorce within the first fifteen years. *Source: American Dating Association 1998 Gender-Normative Long-Term Attitudinal Survey.*

ii. **Applicability**

a. Rules set out in *UDR&B* Sec. IX governing termination of relationships apply to all members of MAD relationships, regardless of the duration of the MAD relationship, the vigor of the relationship, or any other intrinsic or external factors.

b. Rules set out in *UDR&B* Sec. IX governing termination of relationships do not apply to persons who have not pledged sexual exclusivity or in any other way committed themselves to a MAD relationship. *(Note: See* UDR&B *Sec. IV.C.ii.b, regarding the termination of POP relationship.)*

B. **Grounds**

Given that the dissolution of a MAD relationship inevitably brings psychological trauma to one or both members, its dissolution shall not be undertaken without due grounds having been ascertained. Among the grounds considered reasonable for termination purposes:

i. **General Incompatibility.** After the passage of some months or years, a person involved in a romantic relationship may determine that his or her interest in his or her mate is waning.

a. **Indications of waning interest include**

1. The development of pleasant fantasies about what it would be like to live without one's partner.

2. A steady decline in the frequency of sexual relations, to the extent that such relations occur less frequently than the mandated minimum. *(Note: See* UDR&B *Sec.VI.A.ii, "Frequency.")*

3. A persistent lack of interest in a partner's work, hobbies, friends, interests, thoughts, plans, aspirations, or ideas.

4. A frequent feeling of dread at the prospect of seeing, talking to, having sex with, or hearing about one's partner.

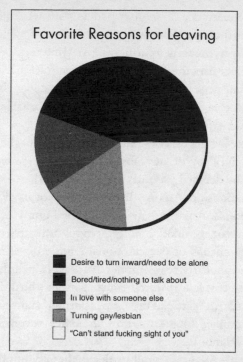

Figure IX.1. Most Often Cited Reasons for Leaving One's Partner. In a survey of 134 couples who had undergone a breakup within the past four weeks, researchers asked what excuse was given by the breaker to the breakee. Of those couples for whom a consistent answer was obtained, a plurality (27 percent) said that the reason was ennui, while nearly as large a proportion cited deepseated hatred and contempt of the breakee as the ostensible motivating factor. *Source:* Sloane, D., and Peterson, N. R., "Causative Factors in Relationship Transition," *Journal of Relationship Psychology,* Vol. XXVI.

5. The existence of another person with whom one would much rather spend one's life.

b. Indications that one's partner is losing interest:

1. Partner uses the word "love" only in reference to physical objects or pets, never to partner.

2. Partner suggests separate vacations, separate beds, or separate habitations.

3. Partner cringes, cries out, or hurries away when touched.

ii. **Neglect.** Neglect of any form is terminally noncompliant and shall be deemed grounds for immediate dissolution of any dating relationship. Among the recognized forms of neglect are

a. **Emotional.** A partner shall be deemed guilty of emotional neglect if he or she takes no interest in his or her partner, has no concern about his or her emotional condition, or in any way projects an appearance of emotional absence, including

1. Persistent failure to remember partner's birthday

2. Persistent failure to remember partner's name

3. Continues to greet with "air kisses" even after many years' relationship

b. **Physical.** A partner shall be deemed guilty of physical neglect if he or she

1. Absents himself or herself for a period of one week or more without notice or explanation

2. Routinely absents himself or herself for three days or more without notice or explanation

3. Gets married and/or moves to another state

iii. **Breach of Trust.** Trust being essential to the preservation of a healthy and compliant dating relationship, its irreparable rupture shall be suitable grounds for the termination of a relationship.

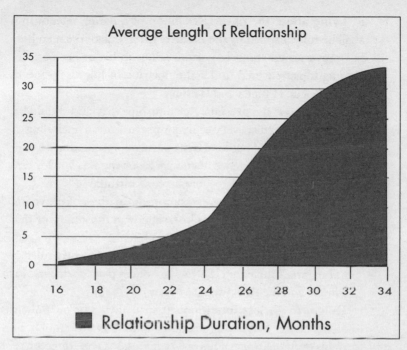

Fig. IX.2. Average Length of MAD Dating Relationships Among American Women. Fifteen hundred single women were surveyed by telephone and asked how long their last sexually exclusive dating relationship lasted. As the results show, relationship duration correlates strongly with age. At age sixteen the average dating relationship lasts just 0.95 months, while by age thirty-four the average duration has risen to a staggering 33 months, or nearly three years. It is interesting to note that by the time she is thirty-four, the average American woman will have gone through fourteen MAD relationships, with a median duration of eight months. *Source:* Freeburg, R. Lynn, "Where the Girls Are: Normative Modes of Self-Perception as Causal Agents for Conceptual Re-Orientation," *Wymyn's Gender Study Initiative,* 1997.

a. **Lying about the past.** Dissolution of a dating relationship shall be fully justified by the discovery that one of the members has prevaricated about important issues in his or her past, including topics covered under the doctrine of full disclosure in *UDR&B* Secs. II.B.iii.a and III.B.iii.

b. **Lying about the present.** Relationships may and should be terminated upon discovery of major prevarication, including

   1. Persistent and habitual lying or misrepresentation on matters of small importance, e.g., why he or she was late for dinner, or why he or she forgot partner's birthday

   2. Any lying or misrepresentation on matters of grave importance, e.g., the fact that he or she won the lottery or that he or she just tested positive for syphilis

   3. Continuing insistence that he or she is deposed ruler of "Hungaria," invented DNA, or once played drums for Hootie and the Blowfish

c. **Failure to disclose intentions.** It shall always be incumbent upon a member of a dating relationship to fully and frankly inform his or her partner of his or her intentions regarding the relationship, and failure to do so shall be grounds for dissolution of said relationship. *Example: John knows that Mary has always dreamed of a lavish wedding. Not until five years into their live-in relationship does he reveal that he never intends to marry. Mary is fully justified in dumping him on the spot. (Note: See* UDR&B *Sec. V.C.ii.b.)*

d. **Failure to handle information.** Concomitant with the responsibility to be honest with one's partner is the responsibility to handle the truth maturely. *(Note: See* UDR&B *Sec. V.B.iv.b.)*

e. **Failure of discretion.** Any person who repeatedly reveals to friends, relatives, or other persons the intimate and private details of his or her dating relationships shall be deemed terminally noncompliant and his or her relationship subject to summary dissolution.

f. **Fiduciary irresponsibility** *(note: see* UDR&B *Sec. VIII.C.i.a)*

g. **Any other act** which might rightly be perceived as a significant breech of trust between partners, including stealing, swindling, and defrauding.

A Closer Look:
Failure to Handle Information

Everyone knows that honesty is a crucial underpinning to any dating relationship. What some people don't realize is that honesty depends on the listener as well as the speaker.

Margaret and Bill had been dating for three months when she asked him, in the course of a romantic evening, where the wildest place he'd ever had sex was. In the spirit of honesty, he told her that he had once had sex on a beach in Mexico.

Inwardly, Bill liked the thought of making love on the beach, and hoped to do it sometime with Margaret. After hearing his tale, however, Margaret became jealous and began criticizing Bill. As their romantic evening devolved into a bickering match, she told him that she might once have wanted to make love on a beach with him, but never would now that she knew he had already done it with some slut.

Margaret's behavior was noncompliant. Being unable to face the truth about Bill's past, she should not have asked. As it was, the potential for an exciting future tryst was ruined.

Dating Tip:
Is It Better to be a Breaker or a Breakee?

The breaker is in charge, and usually gets over the relationship much faster. The breakee gets more sympathy, and can walk away with a sense of righteousness. Which is preferable? It's a judgment call, but overall, 83 percent of all people said that in the abstract, they would prefer to be the breaker. *Source: Compliance Today,* June 1998.

iv. **Infidelity.** Infidelity is terminally noncompliant.

a. The discovery of sexual infidelity shall be understood to invalidate any MAD relationship. *(Note: See UDR&B Sec. V.B, "Exclusivity.")*

1. The discovery of previous sexual interludes between a partner and a third party that predate the establishment of the MAD, and did not extend past it, shall be understood not to constitute infidelity.

2. In the event of infidelity, the partner who commits the offense shall be deemed the "breaker" and the other shall be deemed the "breakee."

b. The following may be taken by a member of a MAD relationship as evidence supporting the possibility that his or her partner is being unfaithful:

1. Partner is suddenly and uncharacteristically happy, for no obvious reason.

2. Partner shows inexplicably renewed enjoyment of and appreciation for life.

3. Partner exhibits sudden and unexplained increase or decrease in sexual appetite.

4. Partner suddenly begins speaking often and glowingly of

a colleague or ostensibly platonic friend of the opposite sex, especially if the other member has never met him or her.

5. Partner begins dressing more fashionably.

6. Partner begins wearing a new fragrance without explanation.

7. Partner suddenly adopts new musical tastes.

8. Incidences of phone hang-ups increase suddenly.

9. Contraceptives or pieces of contraceptive packaging of unknown origin are discovered under furniture.

10. One partner, or both partners, experiences a sudden eruption of venereal disease.

11. Partner becomes pregnant, if male partner is sterile.

c. The following may not be taken as evidence supporting the possibility that one's partner is being unfaithful:

1. Partner frequently looks at members of the opposite sex.

2. Scraps of paper with unfamiliar phone numbers are found in partner's pockets, in partner's wallet, or elsewhere in partner's possession.

3. Incidences of random, isolated, or easily explained phone hang-ups occur.

4. Partner gradually loses interest in sex.

d. If a person has reasonable grounds for believing that his or her partner is being unfaithful, he or she may with good conscience search for evidence among his or her partner's personal effects.

e. Friends

1. No one is obligated to tell a friend that he or she is being cheated upon.

2. A person may not be angry at a friend for not informing him or her of a partner's infidelity.

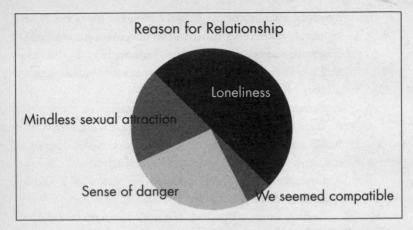

Fig. IX.3. Self-Perception of Rationale for Failed Relationships. One thousand single Americans were asked why they got into their last relationship. Only a very small percentage replied that the likelihood of future compatibility had played a major role in their decision making. *Source:* Edgars, D., "On the Psychodynamics of Romantic Failure," *Nature,* Vol. XVII.

3. A person may not be angry at a friend for informing him or her of a partner's infidelity, if the accusation is true.

v. **Breach of Law.** Criminal malfeasance, whether directed toward one's partner or toward third parties, is terminally noncompliant and shall be grounds for the immediate dissolution of a dating relationship. Such malfeasance includes but is not limited to

a. Punching a nun

b. Joking about bombs at the airport

c. Burning flags in North Carolina

d. Committing hateful speech on college campuses

e. Going to Cuba and buying a lot of cigars

f. Shooting a cute animal, such as Bambi's mom

g. Claiming a full exemption on non-amortizable durable goods held in stock after the beginning of the fiscal year and then deducting interesting expense accrued on line 12 of IRS schedule P, "Other Offshore Finance Charges"

h. Becoming a serial killer and murdering one person for each sign of the zodiac, each deadly sin, each biblical plague, or each team of the American League

i. Any other crime exciting the general contempt and alarm of the community

C. **The Giving of Notice**

A breaker must inform the breakee of the dissolution of the MAD relationship directly and face-to-face, unless the grounds for the breakup is terminal noncompliance such as neglect or infidelity. *(Note: See UDR&B Secs. IX.B.ii and iv.)*

i. **Compliant Modes**

a. Unless physically prevented from achieving physical presence, a breaker must inform the breakee of the relationship's dissolution in person and face-to-face.

b. Having informed the breakee of the relationship's termination, a breaker shall be prepared to spend a long night of

   1. Discussing what went wrong with the relationship

   2. Discussing when things went wrong

   3. Explaining his or her feelings, future plans, and regrets

c. If at all possible, breaker shall not spring news of the breakup on breakee at obviously inconvenient times, e.g., before or during breakee's large birthday party.

d. In discussing reasons for breakup with breakee, breaker will make conscientious effort to minimize psychological damage to the breakee. Such effort may include

1. Accepting blame for the failure of the relationship, even if breaker does not believe it is actually the case
2. Insisting that the breakee is the better person
3. Suggesting that breaker and breakee remain friends, even if breaker has no intention of doing so

ii. **Noncompliant Modes**

a. Breaker shall not inform breakee of the dissolution of the relationship

1. Over the phone

A Closer Look:
Heightening the Contradictions

After spending a good deal of time with someone, the prospect of ruining their happiness, or of making them intensely angry, can never be a pleasant one. To avoid having to initiate a breakup themselves, some people instead resort to a noncompliant dating practice called "heightening the contradictions."

Jake and Marla had been living together for two years when Jake gradually realized that he didn't want to be with her. Their sex life, never good in the best of times, had fallen away to almost nothing. Rather than do the honorable thing, Jake began spending long nights out carousing, taking off on weekend trips without telling Marla, and in general acting like a cad. Miserable, heartbroken, and close to despair, Marla finally had to call it quits.

Jake's cruel strategy might have worked, but in the long run it's Marla who gets the last laugh. She's now a compliant dater, and Jake is not.

2. By letter
3. By facsimile
4. By email, instant messaging, paging, or other electronic media
5. Through a friend or third party
6. By billboard, skywriter, or other form of paid advertisement

b. Breaker shall not attempt to accomplish a relationship's termination by
1. Absenting himself
2. Changing address without informing breakee
3. Never again phoning or taking calls from breakee
4. In any way permanently avoiding breakee

D. **The Split**
i. **Mutual Breakup.** In rare instances, a breakup may be deemed "mutual."
a. **Definition.** If neither party wishes to remain in the relationship, and simultaneously initiate proceedings to effect the dissolution of same, the ensuing breakup may be deemed "mutual."
b. **Rights and responsibilities.** In the event that a breakup shall be deemed by both members of a relationship to have been mutual, both parties shall undertake the responsibilities, but enjoy none of the rights, of the breaker. *(Note: See* UDR&B *Sec. IX.D.ii.a, below.)*
c. **Pseudomutual breakup.** Even if a breakup was not in fact mutual, parties may, by joint agreement, tell friends and family it was mutual for the sake of their own pride and ease of conscience. Each party, however, must still fulfill his or her obligations as breaker or breakee.

ii. **Rights and Responsibilities of the Breaker**
   a. **Responsibilities**

      1. The breaker bears no responsibility if the breakee is guilty of terminal noncompliance such as abuse, neglect, or infidelity. *(Note: See* UDR&B *Secs. IX.B.ii and iv.)*

      2. If there is any ambiguity as to who is the principal owner or leaseholder of the apartment, the breaker shall have the obligation to move out on no more than twelve hours' notice.

      3. The breaker shall bear blame for dissolution of relationship.

      4. If the breakee does not wish it, a breaker shall not contact him or her after the breakup.

      5. Under no circumstances shall the breaker boast, brag, exult, or gloat about having effected the termination of the relationship.

   b. **Rights**

      1. The breaker does not need to observe a mourning period for the terminated relationship.

      2. The breaker may not be contacted by the breakee after the breakup without express permission to do so.

iii. **Rights and Responsibilities of the Breakee**
   a. **Responsibilities**

      1. The breakee may not try to talk the breaker out of his or her decision to terminate the relationship, as by begging, pleading, or threatening.

      2. The breakee may not respond to the breakup with retaliatory measures, such as physical violence, the spreading of false rumors, the leaving of dead pigeons, or the undertaking

of sexual relations with the breaker's friends, colleagues, or family members.

3. The breakee may not attempt to contact the breaker without his or her express and explicit permission.

b. **Rights**

1. The breakee shall be entitled to a mourning period equal to one-half the length of the terminated relationship, or six months, whichever is less. During this time he or she may mope, overeat, cry, feel sorry for himself or herself, and in general behave in a depressed and depressing way, without receiving criticism for it. *(Note: The mourning period should not be confused with the healing period. Mourning ends when a person stops acting out his or her inner pain. Healing ends when a person stops feeling inner pain. The latter generally takes a good deal longer to effect.)*

2. The breakee may not be contacted by the breaker after the breakup without his or her explicit permission.

3. During the mourning period friends and family members shall treat the breakee with special understanding, sympathy, and nurturing kindness.

4. The breakee shall enjoy the knowledge that he or she did his or her best to maintain the relationship despite the unhelpful attitude of the breaker.

E. **Aftermath**

i. **Friends**

a. No person shall expect to maintain cordial relations with the friends, family, or colleagues of an ex-girlfriend or ex-boyfriend, but such cordial relations are permissible.

b. A person shall undertake not to sleep with or begin a romantic relationship with any friend, family member, or colleague of an ex until any of the following has transpired:

1. A period not less than two (2) years has elapsed.
2. The ex has moved out of the state.
3. The ex has married and/or has had children.

c. If in any event the previous rule has been broken, a person shall not brag about the fact to his or her ex.

ii. **Relations with an Ex**

a. **Selectivity of relations.** There shall be no relations whatsoever between exes if either party does not desire it.

b. **Friendship.** If both parties so wish, they may attempt to become platonic friends, so long as each understands that the ease with which a romantic relationship can be converted to a platonic one is inversely proportional to its intensity in the first place.

c. **Stalking**

1. No person shall attempt to follow, spy on, harass, or in any way force his or her presence on an ex.
2. All persons should be aware that many states now carry antistalking laws and that such activities may be punished with lengthy terms of imprisonment.

d. **Recidivism**

1. Former partners shall not undertake to have sexual intercourse with one another following their breakup.
2. Under the Principle of Irreversibility, any future romantic entanglements between exes shall be deemed noncompliant.
(Note: See UDR&B *Sec. V.A.v.c.)*

iii. **Healing**

a. **Posttraumatic promiscuity**

1. Sex with other people is useful for erasing painful memo-

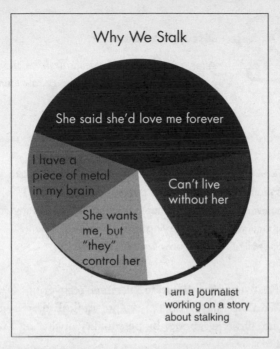

Fig. IX.4. Self-Perceived Motives Among Stalkers. One hundred jailed stalkers were interviewed and asked their motives. A large plurality replied that their former partners had promised them that their love would last forever. Pathetic, really. *Source: Jailbird: The Magazine for Incarcerated Felons, July 1997.*

ries of one's ex, for increasing sexual confidence, and for reminding oneself of an ex's shortcomings.

2. Posttraumatic promiscuity should be practiced with caution, as further psychic trauma may be incurred.

3. Posttraumatic promiscuity shall not be undertaken with old friends, colleagues, or extremely ugly people.

Discussion Points

After reading carefully through Section IX, think about the following questions, or talk them over with a friend:

—In your last relationship, were you the breaker or the breakee? How did it feel?

—Does even thinking about the trauma of breaking up make you want to just bag to the whole relationship thing?

—Did you ever consider that, since a relationship is over anyway, there really isn't much point in worrying about being compliant?

—Did you realize later just how wrong that idea is?

   b. **Restructuring lifestyle.** Persons recovering from a painful breakup may wish to explore radical alterations of their habits, lifestyle, abode, or personality, including but not limited to
      1. Shaving the head
      2. Traveling
      3. Joining the armed forces
      4. Moving to the West Coast *(note: this option is only available to people living east of the Continental Divide; people in the West should not move east, as this will only exacerbate their emotional crisis)*
      5. Crying a lot
   c. **Getting on with life**
      1. Once they feel emotionally prepared, persons recovering from a breakup will find that the greatest measure of relief can be found from entering into another relationship.

2. If the previous relationship was dysfunctional, persons shall attempt to avoid entering relationships characterized by identical dysfunctions.

3. Persons in recovery shall not bore potential partners with stories of the ex-girlfriend or ex-boyfriend.

4. The process of healing officially ends six months into the next relationship. We promise!

Reader Survey

OVERVIEW: *Dating, like life, is not a destination, but a journey. Sometimes the road is rough, sometimes it is smooth. What is most important is to maintain an attitude of curiosity, resilience, and optimism. It is the firm conviction of the American Dating Association that, ultimately, there is the absolutely perfect right someone out there for everyone.*

As you, our cherished scions of the noble tradition of American singlehood, go forth into the great testing ground that is the dating scene, we here at the ADA are standing right behind you, metaphorically if not physically, to help you achieve your dreams of happiness and togetherness with minimal suffering and humiliation. Here we ask you to help us help you by filling out this brief reader survey.

On a scale of 1 to 5, where 5 is "strongly agree" and 1 is "strongly disagree," please rate your response to the following statements about the ADA *2001 Universal Dating Regulations & Bylaws*.

Criterion	1	2	3	4	5
Covered every conceivable dating situation	O	O	O	O	O
Was evidently the work of experts	O	O	O	O	O
Showed years of exhaustive research	O	O	O	O	O
Was highly informational	O	O	O	O	O
Had easy-to-follow layout	O	O	O	O	O

Criterion	1	2	3	4	5
Had nice pictures	○	○	○	○	○
Anticipated my needs as a single heterosexual	○	○	○	○	○
Would richly reward someone who carried it everywhere	○	○	○	○	○
Was much better than the knock-off publication put out by the shoddy rival organization	○	○	○	○	○
Did not need more pictures of nude or seminude people	○	○	○	○	○
Should not have devoted more space to animal rights	○	○	○	○	○
Was not adequately Christian in its outlook	○	○	○	○	○
Made me feel better just by holding it	○	○	○	○	○
Reminded me of something else	○	○	○	○	○
Made me realize what a terrible person my ex was, even though I still really love him/her and always will	○	○	○	○	○
Would have looked better with a blue cover	○	○	○	○	○
Made me sad that anyone would have anything to do with it	○	○	○	○	○
Was obviously made up	○	○	○	○	○

The ADA is a member of the American Federation of Associations.

NOTES

NOTES

NOTES